Kathy —

5/29/01

You said e would
be like a "long, extended vacation" — so
here's to your "second home!"

What doesn't pertain to your
Norway home now may possibly
help with the next overseas "second
home!"

You will never know how
much I will miss you Kathy.

Your friend always,
Julie

Better Homes and Gardens®

secondhome

FINDING YOUR PLACE IN THE FUN

BETTER HOMES AND GARDENS® BOOKS

DES MOINES, IOWA

table of
contents

INTRODUCTION

the MAGIC of it all

ONCE LONELY on the lake shore, this cabin somehow let its future owners know it was waiting to be "adopted." Is your second home waiting for you to find it, too?

4

CHAPTER ONE

DREAM on

THIS TOUR OF CLASSIC COTTAGES—in the woods, on an island, at the seashore, and beside a lake—is designed to stir your own second-home fantasies.

6

CHAPTER TWO

put yourself in the PICTURE

REACT WITH YOUR HEART to the settings in these quizzes. There are no wrong answers—just glimpses of great escapes to help you decide what's right for you.

36

CHAPTER THREE

hit the ROAD

READY TO SHOP FOR YOUR OWN GETAWAY? See how other people found their dream retreats, then use these tips to research the locations you find.

58

BETTER HOMES AND GARDENS® BOOKS
AN IMPRINT OF MEREDITH® BOOKS

SECOND HOME: FINDING YOUR PLACE IN THE FUN
Editor: Denise L. Caringer
Contributing Editor: Sharon Novotne O'Keefe
Contributing Art Director: Kimberly Zarley
Copy Chief: Catherine Hamrick
Copy and Production Editor: Terri Fredrickson
Book Production Managers: Pam Kvitne, Marjorie J. Schenkelberg
Contributing Copy Editor: Carol Boker
Contributing Proofreaders: Kathy Roth Eastman, Nancy Ruhling, Debra Morris Smith
Indexer: Sharon Duffy
Electronic Production Coordinator: Paula Forest
Editorial and Design Assistants: Kaye Chabot, Mary Lee Gavin, Karen Schirm

MEREDITH® BOOKS
Editor in Chief: James D. Blume
Design Director: Matt Strelecki
Managing Editor: Gregory H. Kayko

Director, Retail Sales and Marketing: Terry Unsworth
Director, Sales, Special Markets: Rita McMullen
Director, Sales, Premiums: Michael A. Peterson
Director, Sales, Retail: Tom Wierzbicki
Director, Sales, Home & Garden Centers: Ray Wolf
Director, Book Marketing: Brad Elmitt
Director, Operations: George A. Susral
Director, Production: Douglas M. Johnston

Vice President, General Manager: Jamie L. Martin

BETTER HOMES AND GARDENS® MAGAZINE
Editor in Chief: Jean LemMon
Interior Design Editor: Sandra S. Soria

CHAPTER FOUR

start from
SCRATCH

BEFORE YOU BUILD, look at new home options— custom designs, log and timberframe homes, a stylish modular, and a stock plan you can personalize.

86

CHAPTER FIVE

FIX IT
up

WHEN COTTAGE CHARM IS COVERED by ho-hum siding or dimmed by lack of light, plan a redo to add character outside and to open interiors to the sunlight and the view.

128

CHAPTER SIX

make it
YOURS

DECORATE YOUR SECOND HOME to reflect its location, whether it's by the sea or at the ranch. The two basic ingredients? Comfort and a lighthearted attitude.

166

RESOURCES

sites &
sources

MORE THAN 60 WEBSITES and organizations can help you research locations, get home design help, and find vacation home plans and cottage furnishings online.

212

CREDITS: PAGE 213
INDEX: PAGE 214

Building and Remodeling Editor: Joan McCloskey

MEREDITH PUBLISHING GROUP
President, Publishing Group:
Christopher M. Little
Vice President, Finance and Administration:
Max Runciman

MEREDITH CORPORATION
Chairman and Chief Executive Officer:
William T. Kerr

Chairman of the Executive Committee:
E. T. Meredith III

All of us at Better Homes and Gardens® Books are dedicated to providing you with information and ideas to enhance your home. We welcome your comments and suggestions. Write to us at: Better Homes and Gardens® Books, Shelter Editorial Department, 1716 Locust St., Des Moines, IA 50309-3023.

If you would like to purchase any of our books, check wherever quality books are sold, or visit our website at bhg.com or bhgbooks.com.

Copyright © 2000 by Meredith Corporation, Des Moines, Iowa.

All rights reserved. Printed in the United States of America.
First Edition—00
Library of Congress Catalog Card Number: 00-132134
ISBN: 0-696-21152-1

Cover Photograph: Sam Gray. The home shown is on pages 174-179.

THE magic OF IT ALL

When my husband, Ron, and I were first married, our favorite piece of "artwork" was a prized poster showing a cedar chalet in the woods. Included in a catalog from a company selling pre-cut home kits, the picture represented what was then a distant dream of a rugged little cottage on a lake.

Years passed, and other art soon took the place of that poster, but nothing replaced the dream itself. In fact, every year or two we trekked around our state to hone our second-home vision by looking at everything from acreages with ponds to lake homes. Even vacation trips included the inevitable real estate search: How about a cottage in Sausalito? A condo in Maui? A little place in Key West? A lakefront getaway in the Ozarks? A townhouse in Palm Springs? In those travels, we scooped up dreams, as well as information. And we talked—oh, did we talk—about locations, home styles, furnishings, and what our ideal setting might be.

And then one spring it all came together. We decided that what we really needed was a regular weekend escape—a place close enough so that, in the summertime, we could be lounging on our own lakeside dock by sunset on a Friday evening. What happened next is strange but true: I had a dream that our ideal second home was out there somewhere, if only we could find it. Trusting the dream, we began our hunt in earnest. Just a few weeks later, we found the perfect lakefront A-frame—and it had been put on the market the very week I'd dreamed of it.

Since then, I've come to think of our little lake house as a kind of Velveteen Rabbit—a place so often and lovingly used that it has become "real." To us, it's not just a place but a beloved member of the family. In fact, I'm so happy to get "home" to it on Friday evenings that I'd put my arms around the entire house and hug it if only I could.

When I consider the stories of all the homeowners featured in this book, I wonder: Grand or modest, what is it about second homes that touches us so? Why is it that perfectly normal adults who suit up for work and act their age Monday through Friday find themselves chasing each other across the yard with squirt guns on Saturday? What is it about a second-home location that moves us to lie, childlike, in the grass to look for constellations at night—or hop out of bed much too early in the morning just to see the sun rise? Why do little things seem so special? Morning coffee becomes an occasion when we're on the dock with our feet dangling lazily in the water.

Whatever their sizes, locations, or price tags, these getaways—where phone calls are few and junk mail never arrives—offer a special sense of enchantment and an opportunity to reawaken a childlike sense of play that gets lost in the workaday world of traffic snarls, ringing phones, crowded airplanes, crammed schedules, missed lunches.

You don't have to share my attitude about our A-frame retreat—a cottage that others might drive by without a second glance. The point of this book is for you to clarify your own vision—and make it real. You can start the process right now, because this book is designed not only to help you plan your own great escape but to let you relax, dream, and get away simply by turning the pages. Along the way, we'll help you consider location, home style, your lifestyle, financing, and all the other essentials, but we've included big beautiful photos of homes and great settings to help you sense the fun and *magic* of it all. That sense of magic makes me believe that our little A-frame, standing lonely and empty on the shore, somehow came to me in a dream to let me know it was waiting for us to "adopt" it. Is your second home out there somewhere just waiting for you to find it, too?

Denise L. Caringer

Denise L. Caringer
Editor, *Second Home*

DREAM on

When you want to get away from it all, where does your heart lead you? For some, it's a shore thing for beachcombing and romantic sunsets. Others take the first backwoods exit to solitude. Whether there's a mountaintop or a rural hamlet in your daydreams, the perfect spot for a getaway home is any place that renews your spirit and lets you do the things you love. The homeowners in this chapter knew their psyches and their needs before they chose their locations. Now, on weekends, they head off in different directions—to the woods, the lake, an island, or the seashore. Come along on a tour designed to stir your own dreams.

RIGHT: Cedar Lake beckons behind Mickey and Tom Harris's Oklahoma cabin, featured on the following pages. A canoe is always ready so the couple can fish for supper or simply paddle out to drift with the wind.

THE BIG WOODS

Sometimes, it's easy to pass up paradise in search of a getaway. If you'd rather spend the weekend with a deck chair and a good book instead of a hammer (who wouldn't?), the fixer-upper may not be for you. Then again, it may be your perfect getaway in disguise if the location is right. That's what Mickey and Tom Harris of Tulsa, Oklahoma, realized when they first laid eyes on a one-room, vintage-1934 log cabin that had grown with makeshift add-ons over time. What clinched the deal was the wooded site on a peaceful lake within driving distance of home. And they figured that by phasing in needed remodeling and decorating changes over several years, they could ensure plenty of relaxation time. The plan worked.

"We fished really hard the first 10 years," Tom says. "We still love to fish, but we'd just as soon sit on the porch and watch for deer. We still consider it a getaway from the city, but rather than isolating ourselves, we spend more time now with friends."

Guided by their love of Country French antiques, the couple transformed the forlorn cabin into a charming French farmhouse, inside and out. They replaced blond wall paneling and acoustical ceiling tiles with honey-hued pine planks and rugged beams. Original pine floors, once hidden under carpet, were restored, and the couple scrounged through attics and lumberyards for traditional wood windows to replace aluminum sliders. Consummate collectors,

OPPOSITE: Tom laid a welcoming entry path of stone. **ABOVE:** New upholstered seating gathers around a primitive 1860 trunk. Airy botanical prints lighten the cabin's interior. **RIGHT:** A section of stucco blends the cabin's patchwork of additions.

they mixed antiques and reproduction furnishings. An early 18th-century painted armoire with gathered fabric and chicken wire insets forms a living room focal point, while new upholstered seating offers modern-day comfort.

With a massive stone fireplace and exposed walls, the cabin's original log room formed a rustic touchstone in the redesign because, with only new windows, it remains essentially unchanged. Fresh country fabrics, inviting colors, sink-in seating, and personality collections take the primitive edge off the space. In fact, one look at the over-size ottoman, and there's no mistaking the fact that comfort tops the couple's design agenda. Sharing their retreat with friends is part of the fun, so the dining room features an ample antique farm table—a $40 find from an old Missouri building—surrounded by 10 circa-1890 French chairs repainted yellow.

"Tom used the table as a workbench for years, then we realized that the tin top was actually pretty cool, so we moved it into the dining room," says Mickey.

The charms of the past often don't carry over to aging kitchens. As Mickey says, the novelty of cooking over a wood stove in the 1930s kitchen quickly wore off. Doing much of the work themselves, the Harrises created a French farmhouse kitchen with a modern stove and dishwasher flanked by painted wood cabinetry and stonelike concrete counters. A wrought-iron table serves as an island, as well as a style bridge linking the functional with the romantic. To preserve the cabin's original look, the couple added new windows that reproduce the style and aged finish of the room's original panes.

OPPOSITE and ABOVE: Antiqued metal hardware and an earthy array of baskets, spices, vinegars, and oils age and countrify the remodeled kitchen.
RIGHT: A claw-foot tub and pine paneling lend cabin style to a new bath.

UNDERSTANDING YOUR PSYCHE

Second-home locations are inherently inspiring, so emotions can run high when you shop
for a getaway. To make the best choice, shop with a clear vision of what you *really* want.

▦ What hobbies do you want to indulge or develop? Does your dream include great fishing, as
the Harrises' did, or perhaps a nearby town dotted with antiques shops or a great flea market?

▦ Do you crave peace—or partying? With serenity at the top of their list, the Harrises chose a
lake that allows only canoes and johnboats with trolling motors. No noisy jet skis!

▦ How often do you plan to get away? It's easy to "vacation" every weekend if you choose a
site that's a two- or three-hour drive from home.

▦ How much light do you need? A log cabin in the woods is fine if you fantasize about Davy
Crockett's wild frontier. If you lean toward light and airy, think bright beach house, instead.

ABOVE: A new fireplace and snug wing chairs add bed-and-breakfast charm to the refurbished
bedroom. A French limestone mantel, French doors, a painted floor, and a vaulted ceiling clad in
old fencing enhance the old-world look. **RIGHT:** Antique garden tools accent the screen porch
that's set comfortably for dining, relaxing, and deer watching.

SAND AND sea

I s it wing tips or flip-flops? What you stuff into your beach bag determines how much you enjoy a trip to the shore. The same holds true when packing amenities into a beach home. Leave the buttoned-down rules back home, as the owners of this home near Wellfleet, Massachusetts, did. Taking liberties with classic Cape Cod design, they chose vaulted ceilings for volume and large windows for wraparound seascapes.

ABOVE: Cedar shingle siding that weathers without upkeep on this seaside home has been a Cape Cod tradition since Colonial times.
LEFT: Centrally located in the open plan, the dining area opens to a deck.
OPPOSITE: Creamy colors and muted patterns keep the living room mood serene. Pale hues and rattan accents visually link the interiors with the sandy setting.

Wisely, the couple didn't design just for today. They looked to retirement, too. A bedroom wing for visiting family and guests can be closed off. Main living spaces—the kitchen, dining area, living room, and an enclosed porch— enjoy the best ocean views, and the home's one-level design keeps the interior step- and barrier-free.

The all-in-one dining area and kitchen gathers the family together for good cooking and lively conversation— just the kind of memory-making times they envisioned. Friendly finishes, such as beadboard paneling and rich oak floors, create a warm, informal backdrop for the comfort-cued blend of new and old furnishings.

LEFT: A built-in desk and island boost the kitchen's efficiency. **ABOVE:** Curling up with a book by the toasty fireplace is a rainy-day option. **OPPOSITE:** The island's eating counter supplements the trestle table when there's a crowd for dinner.

Raised ceilings make the home feel roomier than it is. The homeowners pared down floor space by designing rooms to hold only priority furniture pieces. The 13x14-foot master bedroom, for instance, is big enough for a queen-size bed, dresser, nightstand, and wicker chair—but no more. The couple chose simple window treatments to keep the focus on the bedroom's beautiful views. The lure of outdoor living is irresistible with a private deck off the master bedroom, the main deck off dining and living rooms, and a rain-or-shine screen porch.

TOP: Indigenous trees and naturalized plantings create a no-mow landscape. **ABOVE:** The master bedroom deck has a built-in bench for lounging. **OPPOSITE:** With a protective roof overhead, the screen porch offers the comfort of wicker seating pieces cushioned in a seashell-print fabric.

AN ISLAND ESCAPE

When it comes to personal style, you can take it with you, even if your retreat or retirement dream home includes downsized spaces. As they settled into their Saint Simons Island, Georgia, home, Polly and Tom Minick imbued their country furnishings with fresh spirit by letting go and having fun. To pare down, they chose a red, white, and blue scheme, then sold anything that didn't fit it.

LEFT: Airedales, Pepper and Dixie, lounge beneath a rug Polly designed. **ABOVE:** Old signs and crocks top an 1800s apothecary chest. **TOP:** The home's classic styling suits the couple's American antiques.

ABOVE: Vegetable dyes in the accessories' aged paints produce softly varied shades of reds and blues that relax the mood. **OPPOSITE:** White walls and a few bold furnishings make short work of living room decorating.

Realizing that the home's coastal setting and strong sun called for a breezier take on country decorating, Polly combined her collector's appreciation for the past with a newfound desire for rooms that are open, airy—and simply fun. "I really wanted to go lighter, brighter, and more sparse," she explains. The couple's 19th-century American furniture and folk-art accents, such as the flag wall hanging above the living room fireplace, make a bolder, more graphic statement against the gallery-white walls. Imperfections of age make the painted furniture charming and easy to live with because a nick or scrape doesn't matter. In fact, Polly insists that refinishing a piece "takes the story right off of it."

Less space and a more laid-back lifestyle left no room for anything that was fussy or frivolous, and Polly vetoed window treatments in the dining room because they would detract from the furnishings. Sturdier than most antiques, the sawbuck table and Windsor chairs are new reproductions, as is the blue cupboard that's outfitted with old doors. With an eye on comfort, upholstered seating throughout is also new. "I'm for the look and what works for our family," Polly says. She indulges her love of early American textiles, including wool blankets and ticking, by sewing them into bed skirts and pillow shams and by stacking them for pattern punch in an old cupboard in the master bedroom.

OPPOSITE: Vintage textiles, linked by blue and white, dress the canopy bed in the master bedroom. **RIGHT:** A reproduction table and chairs blend in spirit with the antique accents. **BELOW:** Fresh white paint pulls together a friendly collection of mismatched wicker.

CREATING ROOM TO BREATHE

Let the Minicks inspire your own breezy, less-is-more philosophy.

▨ Edit wisely. Pare your collections for clutter-free interiors.

▨ White's right. Colors and textures pop against the white backdrops that make rooms feel simpler, cleaner, more relaxed.

▨ Undress windows. Shutters make good replacements for fussy fabric window treatments.

▨ Add carefully. Buy an antique only if you have a place for it.

▨ Use see-through furniture, such as rod-back Windsors, a trestle table, and a virtually bare canopy bed, to foster an airy look.

LAKESHORE GETAWAY

Remember camping out as kids, snuggling and giggling in a pup tent pitched in a wilderness that, by day, looked exactly like the backyard? Roughing it is fun, but everybody defines it differently. Back then, the cookies and comforts of home were steps away from the pup tent. Wherever you set up a second-home camp, you can take comfort along, too, and still walk on the wild side.

Marc and Anne Margulies didn't stray far from their Boston home when they chose a New Hampshire lake site for their new retreat. It's two hours away, so they often drive up on weekends. Simplicity and sunrises guided Marc, an architect, as he nestled the east-facing home among the trees. Cozy interiors share sylvan and White Mountains views, but he saved the best lake vista for the great-room where everybody gathers around the fieldstone fireplace.

LEFT: High-rise windows overlooking the lake make the great-room a favorite spot for family and friends to get together and relax on pillow-strewn leather sofas, a sunny window seat, and an antique twig chair. **RIGHT:** White painted pine defines the lakeside windows. A mix of stained shingles and green clapboards lends cottage style. **FAR RIGHT:** In a woodsy setting like this, table decor is as simple as a birch bark basket filled with plants.

With three children and lots of guests, the couple designed main living spaces that flow together so folks cooking up the day's catch in the kitchen still feel connected to conversation in the great-room. The dining area, with walls painted forest green and deep blue, is a pivotal point between the great-room and kitchen, and offers fantastic lake views although the home is sited 300 feet from the shore to preserve wetlands. "The house has no sense of grandeur," Marc says. "It's meant to be welcoming, cozy, and relaxing."

The large open kitchen with pine-plank ceiling and open shelves looks as if it were plucked from an old Adirondack camp, but it works efficiently with a butcher-block worktable, easy-care laminate countertops, and a backsplash of textured paint. "I told Marc I didn't want a home that felt like a condo," says Anne. "I wanted a rustic place that was easy to maintain, smallish yet able to absorb a lot of people. I come from a big family."

OPPOSITE: A red-gold stain gives the kitchen's pine ceiling a warm, natural look. Wrought-iron cabinet hardware in frog, turtle, fish, and leaf shapes adds whimsy.
ABOVE RIGHT: An antique farm table teams up with reproduction straw-seat chairs in the lake-view dining room.

PLANNING FOR A CROWD

Part of the fun of getting away for the weekend is bringing family and friends along for outdoor activities, leisurely feasts, and relaxed conversation. To plan your getaway, adapt this home's welcoming ideas.

◈ The large, open living-dining area encourages community. In a slice of space, a long dining table can seat a crowd—or host a buffet dinner.

◈ Multiple work areas in the kitchen give family and guests a chance to relax, visit, and cook together.

◈ A built-in window seat supplements great-room seating.

◈ The bunk room and loft can sleep eight overnight guests.

◈ The screen porch is big enough to combine two tables for 18 diners.

LEFT: Inherently relaxing, the master bedroom's blue wall echoes the color of the lake and sky. Treasures include a tribal runner from Pakistan, where Marc lived as a child, and a pillow with a picture of the lake—a Mother's Day gift from the children. **BELOW:** Beneath the interior leaded-glass window, an English pine chest stows clothes. **OPPOSITE:** Railed overlooks allow light to flow from great-room windows into the bunk room and loft.

Designing and furnishing the retreat was a family affair. Marc handled the plans with Anne in the "client" role, and he also made much of the furniture with the help of their children, Jeff, Tucker, and Kendra, who invite friends to join the family on weekends. The bunk room at the top of the stairs sleeps four, and up a retractable ladder is a loft that sleeps four more. Nobody misses a lake view because the bunk room overlooks the great-room's tall windows. Built-in open shelves and hooks on the bunks replace closets.

Marc also built the cottage-style bed that's showcased against red and blue walls in the master bedroom. There's no need for window treatments in this treetop retreat, and furnishings such as the Adirondack chair and twig table are rustic and practical. Even though the master bedroom doesn't face the lake, it still captures a view. "We can actually see water through the leaded-glass interior window that faces the windows in the great-room," Anne says.

Outdoor living spaces are roomy enough for entertaining. But, thanks to antique rockers on the deck and handcrafted Adirondack chairs on the dock, there are plenty of quiet spots for reading or watching the water. Marc built the Philippine mahogany chairs, then angled the dock for a special view. "When you sit on it, you're looking down the lake directly at Mount Kearsarge," he explains.

Between the kitchen and dining area, a doorway leads to the screen porch—a second eating area the family often uses for mosquito-free summer parties. When the porch's redwood table isn't big enough to seat everyone, they tote out the dining area's farm table and turn the two into a T-shape table that seats 18.

LEFT: With chairs for relaxing, the angled dock is both a fishing spot and a perch for enjoying the mountain view down the lake. **ABOVE:** Instead of buying a ready-made redwood table for the screen porch, Marc built one to the desired size and shape. **OPPOSITE:** The deck offers front-row seats for watching lake activities and for rocking away a lazy afternoon.

put yourself
in the
PICTURE

Close your eyes and imagine a place that relaxes you, energizes your spirit, and inspires freedom and fun. Think of it as your soul mate with a ZIP code. Is paradise a powdered-sugar beach, a desert mesa, a mountain lake? Is it on a rural route or in the city? This fun chapter will help you decide which second-home location is right for you. For starters, click off that busy brain for a few moments and react with your heart to the getaway places shown in the mini quizzes on the following pages. There are no right or wrong answers and no scoring—just a little prompting to help you envision yourself in a variety of settings.

RIGHT: Do weekends get any better than this? Instantly relaxing, a wild-blue-yonder view of water and sky is sure to inspire flights of fancy. The take-off point for this solitary sunbather is the beach near Union Pier, Michigan.

PICK AN aTMOSPHere

It's 8 a.m. at your enchanted forest cottage, but your wake-up call isn't the chirping birds you expected. It's the whine of jet skis racing around the lake just beyond your deck. To avoid surprises and disappointments after you buy a second home, be sure you know what kind of atmosphere relaxes and rejuvenates you. Then visit your location on weekends, weekdays, at various times of the day, and in on- and off-seasons to get the feel of the place.

Ask yourself what kinds of settings appeal to you. Are you drawn to bright, sunny beaches? Do deep, dark woods make you feel safe, cozy or claustrophobic? What climates do you enjoy? Do you crave crisp, snowy days, year-round tropical sun, or rainy days for fireside cocooning? Do you like familiarity or adventure? For some, a city makes the ideal getaway. What about a pied-à-terre in Chicago or New York for shopping, theater, and museums?

LEFT: Know yourself: Would a cottage with a sunny, secluded garden dining spot like this be too hot, too hard on your allergies, too claustrophobic—or just right?

TRY OUT LOCATIONS

- If possible, visit a potential getaway location for two or more years in a row.
- Camp out on that mountain site you're thinking of buying.
- Take home-swap vacations to check out different locales.
- Take a virtual vacation, touring homes and locations on the Internet.
- Near a golf course? Check out how easy it is to drive, walk, or cart over to it.

IN YOUR SECOND-HOME DREAM, WHERE ARE YOU WALKING?

Through a lush and fragrant garden or orchard?

Along a snowy path in the woods?

On a lush carpet of grass at the golf course?

Barefoot in warm sand at the beach?

WHAT'S YOUR STYLE?

After a hectic workweek, you dream of taking off for a well-deserved respite at your second home. Before you shop for that great escape, clarify your vision, and check it with your partner or spouse. Is it a mountain cabin? A shingle-style Victorian with an ocean-view porch? A fuss-free contemporary condo? What's on your must-have list of features? Wood-beamed ceilings? A deck or patio for dining? A master bedroom terrace? A screen porch? A bunk room for the kids? A big kitchen? Whatever the style, be sure your second home offers the spaces to do whatever you love. After all, that's the point of a getaway.

TEST YOUR "VISION"

Are you and your partner or spouse on the same page when it comes to second-home style? Assign yourselves different color sticky notes, then go through this book and mark homes or rooms you like. Discuss your definitions of cozy, warm, comfy, and relaxing, then look for compromises. Rustic traditionalists and light-and-airy fans can coexist if you paint walls white and leave beams natural, team a stone fireplace with white paneling, or panel walls in light pine and bring in lots of airy wicker and canvas furnishings.

IN YOUR IMAGINATION, WHEN YOU ARRIVE AT YOUR IDEAL GETAWAY, WHAT TYPE OF HOME DO YOU WANT TO SEE?

A lake house, complete with its own boat and dock?

A Southwestern adobe house with big-sky views?

A small-town cottage with its own blooming garden?

A rugged chalet set for skiing and snowshoeing?

A classic cabin encircled by deep woods?

Anything—as long as it has an ocean view?

HOW'S THE view?

Second-home shoppers take the scenic route, and views usually reign in the locations they choose, building sites they buy, and homes they design or remodel. Here are some questions to consider as you plan your getaway. Which views inspire you? Ocean waves, a glimpse of lake through the trees, a city skyline by night? Will a glimpse of water satisfy you? Today, beachfront and lakefront properties come at premium prices, some up to 20 times more than comparable landlocked properties. A less costly landward lot with an unobstructed water view or a home within walking distance of the beach may suit you—or be a disappointment in the long run. If beach or lake frontage is too pricey, but you want a water view, consider a river site but head for higher ground for overviews, breezes, and safety from floods.

Do you like long or short views? Some find vistas of open water, rolling hills, or desert landscapes pleasing; others find them boring. A cabin set amid tall trees is cozy to some, too confining for others.

Are you a sunrise or a sunset fan? The answer could determine which side of a lake or mountain you choose—and could influence your home's design.

Finally, challenge your ideas about the kind of site you want: For instance, with neighbors right across the water, that supposedly quiet, narrow lake cove may be noisy on weekends. Or, if you've dreamed of a lake view, might river frontage work just as well?

THE PERFECT SCENE FROM YOUR FANTASY HIDEAWAY IS:

A picturesque marina filled with sailboats?

A rugged landscape including distant mountains or hills?

Your own swimming pool overlooking the countryside?

A rural farmhouse porch leading to a private backyard?

An intimate garden with its own small pond?

A lofty balcony with a big-water view?

CROWDS VS. SOLITUDE

ABOVE: Be honest about your personality type, and plan your getaway to accommodate it. Ask yourself: Do I need to get away from the group—or join the crowd—to reenergize? Here, a skier glides along a pristine wilderness trail on Drummond Island, Michigan, a quiet spot accessible only by ferryboat.

Sanctuary. Regeneration. Communing with nature. Those are great reasons to head for the log cabin on the lake, the old farmhouse in an apple orchard, or the barrier-island cottage. How many people will be coming along, and how difficult will it be to find solitude—if that's what you want—after you get there? As you think about locations, home designs, and sites, consider how much togetherness you really want. Do you prefer quiet weekends? A romantic retreat for two? Do you want a family getaway with children and friends traipsing in and out?

Some locations seem to epitomize tranquility, but looks can be deceiving. For instance, if you build or buy a home on a public beach, you could be sitting on your deck and bidding "good morning" to a daily parade of beachcombers.

Before you buy, also check the zoning of neighboring properties: Could a condominium project or a new strip mall or a restaurant change the quiet character and view? If you're considering a popular resort area, visit during the tourist season to see how crowded roads, shops, ski lifts, and restaurants will be.

WHEN YOU THINK ABOUT BUYING A SECOND HOME, WHAT DO YOU LOOK FORWARD TO MOST?

Inviting friends and family for a busy day on the water?

Private moments for the two of you—and maybe Fido, too?

Joining a group for hiking, skiing, or partying?

Being alone with your thoughts—and a serene view?

WHAT'S HAPPENING?

Even if everything about the weekend cottage you buy is perfect, civilization will beckon sooner or later. What services, activities, and amenities do you want? Is a town within driving distance? How far are the grocery and hardware stores, library, hospital, pharmacy, movie theater, and gas station? Are there antiques shops, flea and farmers' markets, and local festivals? What's the range of restaurant fare? Are there tourist spots, such as state parks and historical sites? If you look for an area offering a variety of activities, you can learn to sail, hike a mountain, catch the dogsled races, or simply dive into a pile of best-sellers on a rainy day.

LEFT: Check out the towns within driving distance of second-home locations you are considering. On a Saturday morning you can take off for a little antiques shopping in towns, such as Loudonville, Ohio, and still be snoozing in the sun by noon. **TOP:** Nearby farmer's markets can be just the spot for family fun—and fresh produce. **ABOVE:** Local festivals, like this art fair in Burlington, Iowa, along the Mississippi River, add a fresh and fun dimension to a second home. **OPPOSITE:** Tucked amid hills, valleys, and bluffs from coast to coast, picturesque towns, such as Stillwater, Minnesota, on the St. Croix River, invite exploration.

HOW WOULD YOU DESCRIBE FUN AT YOUR PERFECT GETAWAY?

Hanging out with the family on an ample dock perched above the water?

Ice fishing on a frozen lake?

Pedaling down a rural lane?

Learning to dogsled in backcountry?

Lounging by the pool and spa?

Snoozing in a shaded hammock?

Speeding cross-country on a snowmobile?

Gathering friends for a day of fishing?

Kayaking to see the local sights?

Enjoying serene walks with the family?

Setting out on horseback for an afternoon ride and picnic?

Planning and tending your own country garden?

HOW Near, HOW Far?

Where in the world is that idyllic spot for your second home? Down the road or a plane ride away? It depends on your leisure and vacation style.

Do you want to go the distance—or not? Part of the second-home fun is entertaining, so think, too, about how far your guests may be willing to drive to see you.

What is your preferred vacation length? Do you like fewer but longer breaks, such as monthlong vacations? Do you have summers off for extended visits to, say, a cottage in Ireland or a farm home in Provence? Or, do you crave lots of long-weekend "vacations"?

If you want to get to the lake for a sunset cruise on Friday evening, shop within 300 miles—or less—of your primary home. A getaway no more than an hour or so away also can extend your weekend if you commute to work on Monday morning. A close-to-home retreat is ideal if you want a spot where your kids can regularly entertain friends from home.

OPPOSITE: A colorful hammock and sling chairs create a pretty and practical backyard focal point for a land-locked site. **RIGHT:** Fuss-free, portable chaises make it easy to enjoy a beach-front location.

SHOP THE CIRCLE

Decide how far you want to drive to your second home. Then, spread out a state road map and draw a circle around your primary home to designate that distance. If you want to limit the drive to two hours, look for a place 130 miles or less from home. Once you see which counties your circle includes, go to each for a county map to pinpoint such features as private lakes and golf courses. Armed with that information, you can shop the circle for your own piece of paradise.

BEYOND THE WEEKEND reTReaT

Does spending more than the occasional weekend at your cottage figure into your plans? Maybe it should. After all, change happens. Taking retirement or early retirement, buying a home-based business, or telecommuting can open up new possibilities for enjoying your second home. So as you shop, keep in mind that the right location and the right home could be the long-term answer to change—planned or unexpected—that may come your way.

If you're eyeing a second home as a potential home office, home-based business, or retirement spot, select one with enough square footage to accommodate your future needs or one that can be remodeled. Check zoning restrictions to see if it's legal to operate a home business in your area. Telecommuters need efficient office space, and home-based businesses may need work and conference space for client meetings.

For retirement, build in play space for hobbies and the grandchildren, add zoned climate controls to shut off unused guest quarters, and consider a location with a bustling town nearby.

ABOVE: To plan for retirement, minimize steps and consider one-level living. **OPPOSITE:** An inviting multilevel home can serve long-term retirement needs if you include a main-level master suite.

RETIREMENT REALITY CHECK

Today, more retirees are following the trend to call small college towns—even the old alma mater—home. In evaluating a retirement location, consider: What's the quality and accessibility of health care? Is the area safe, the crime rate low? What's the cost of living? Are there opportunities for part-time work? What are the cultural and educational offerings, such as Elder Hostel programs? Are there indoor and outdoor sports venues? Is the climate comfortable?

HOW MUCH CAN YOU afford?

Before you begin serious shopping for a second home, set a realistic home price range and stick to it. It's easy to get swept away by an ocean view or a charming cottage complete with picket fence and bay window.

To calculate the cost of living in a second home, make a copy of your household budget for your primary residence and fill in the estimated costs of the same items at your second home. Groceries and gasoline often cost more in resort locations. Total the estimates for food, travel, homeowner's insurance, utilities, upkeep, and security or property management, if needed. Figure the price of any remodeling changes you may need to make. Research state and local property taxes. Add hidden costs, such as special flood or hurricane insurance. Lenders may require a larger down payment in some second home locations. If you plan to make your cottage your primary home someday, will your car, home, and health insurance rates change? Find out how a second home affects your tax situation, especially if you are considering retiring to a second home in another state.

TIPS ON TAXES

How much you use or rent a vacation home determines what you're able to deduct from your taxes. Under current federal tax regulations, if you and your family use the house fewer than 14 days a year (or 10 percent of the total time it's rented), it's considered a rental property. That means you can deduct most of your expenses in maintaining it. Use the house for more than that and it's considered a residence, and your expenses can't exceed your income from the property. If you rent fewer than 15 days a year, you don't have to report the income.

ABOVE: Second homes come in all sizes and budgets. How about a condo with a great view? **LEFT:** A spacious cottage on a lake gathers family and friends in style.

FINANCIAL OPTIONS

How will you fund the purchase of a second home? It's a good idea to get some answers before you start shopping. The sizable number of cash buyers in the second-home market have the edge. But if you're not one of them, getting mortgage preapproval before you launch your search will keep you competitive if you find a hot property. For quick cash, borrowing from the cash value of a whole-life insurance policy is one option, as long as you set up a repayment plan to preserve the policy's long-term value.

Shop around for the best interest rate if you want a fixed-rate mortgage on the property. Depending on how long you plan to own the property, consider exploring adjustable-rate mortgages with, for example, fixed interest and monthly payments for five to seven years. If sellers own the property outright, ask if they would consider seller financing. You may be able to negotiate a lower interest rate, a lower down payment, and a flexible payment plan.

RENTING OUT YOUR RETREAT

One way to defray the costs of owning a second home is to rent it out when your family isn't using it. Here are some things to consider:

▨ If the home is in a development with a homeowners association, ask if you're allowed to rent out your home. The answer may be no.

▨ Limit wear and tear by renting only by the month or the season.

▨ Use word-of-mouth advertising; rent to friends (or friends of friends) who may be more likely than strangers to treat your place with care.

▨ It takes time to handle inquiries and deal with potential renters yourself. Is it worth the expense of hiring a rental manager who will schedule renters, and handle emergencies and maintenance?

▨ You may want to add amenities, such as hot tubs, televisions, gas grills, and a modern kitchen, to keep renters coming back. You'll also want a locked storage room or closet for your family's possessions.

ABOVE: Budget strategy: Buy a great view, insist on a deck, but adjust home plans to cut costs. **OPPOSITE:** Pricey details—masonry fireplaces, lots of wood—add up fast.

hit the road

Stress relief. Status. Fun. Retirement. Investment. These are the dreams that lure shoppers into the second-homes market. And it's getting crowded out there as more people put a vacation home at the top of their wish lists. Expectations run high, but don't lose the dream by rushing the decision. Although your first impulse may be to head for distant mountains or seas, you may find yourself buying into one of the biggest trends—finding a close-to-home getaway for regular weekend jaunts. Brake for a reality check and do your homework to be sure your lifestyle and location are a perfect match.

RIGHT: In the Northwest, a scenic ferry ride takes second-home shoppers to sites on nearby islands. This ferry links Vancouver to Bowen Island, British Columbia, a 20-minute trip.

A SOUND INVESTMENT

Whether you take to the highway or the Internet's superhighway, profile locations to answer important long-term questions. It's a great vacation spot, but what's it really like to live there? Does it offer activities and adventures to grow with your family? What's the area's economic outlook? As empty nesters, will you still love it? Does its special character make you feel like, for the money, there's no place you'd rather be?

Even sentimental favorites—the old hometown, that great fishing lake, or the annual ski destination—need objective, in-depth research when investment's on the line. Childhood memories of seaside summers lured Pam Christensen back to Fenwick, Connecticut, on Long Island Sound. It hadn't changed much, and that was a plus. So was the price tag. The 1920s bungalow Pam and her husband, Bill, rescued was in tear-down shape, but affordable.

ABOVE: A new addition doubled the size of this seaside shingled bungalow, and renovation put it in sync with its larger Victorian neighbors. **LEFT:** Once the living room's dated textured ceilings were removed, fresh paint and stock moldings gave the room timeless appeal.

For the Christensens, the bungalow was a wise investment because it's close to their primary home in New York City, they love beach living, and Fenwick is as charming today as it was a century ago when city folks first summered there.

Pam, an interior designer, joined forces with her sister, Brooke Girty, the project architect, in the renovation that rebuilt the bungalow's character inside and out, captured views with new windows, and doubled the square footage with a two-story addition at the back for a master bedroom, kitchen, dining room, and two porches.

To fit their casual living and entertaining style, the furnishings are relaxed, durable, and easy to clean or shake out when the weekend is over. Seating is slipcovered, and rag rugs and straw mats cover fir floors. Pam's palette of sandy beiges and crisp whites doesn't compete with the views. The summer-loving sisters met their design goal: Create a welcoming home where everybody feels comfortable.

OPPOSITE: An ogee arch turns bunk beds into an exotic hideaway for the couple's daughter, Olivia, and friends. **ABOVE:** The addition's master bedroom has floor-to-ceiling beadboard walls and a window seat with a special lighthouse view.

PROTECTING YOUR INVESTMENT

Research the area to be sure that your potential retreat's view, access, or tranquility is not on the endangered list.

▣ What growth is rumored, expected, or planned in the area? Chat with would-be neighbors and check city and county planning offices for possible development or zoning changes.

▣ Are there upcoming road projects or environmental designations? State highway and natural resources offices know.

▣ Are nearby homes well kept, or do they look neglected?

WORKING WITH CITY HaLL

Wide-open spaces aren't for everybody. From the north woods and farm country to the seashore, small towns can offer second-home shoppers that coveted change of pace, plus a sense of community. If you yearn to ease into small-town life and build on an infill lot, be a good neighbor by pleasing city hall and creating a design that nods to local architectural traditions.

When Kathleen and Mark Sullivan decided to retire in their favorite vacation spot, Capitola, California, fitting a home onto a 50x50 lot was a challenge. By designing a new home that fits the look of the neighborhood and obeys the town's tough building codes, architect Tobin Dougherty created a cottage that looks as if it has always been there.

CHECK OUT THE NEIGHBORHOOD

▣ What is the cost of living? How much have home values risen? Are there property tax breaks for seniors?

▣ Visit the area on weekends and weekdays. Get out of the car, take a walk, and listen: Is it too noisy, too quiet, or just right?

▣ Learn what cultural, educational, and recreational offerings—colleges, sports, libraries, theaters, restaurants, shops—are nearby.

▣ Is health care close by? Are fire and police coverage adequate?

▣ How far are the pharmacy, gas station, grocery and hardware stores?

▣ Are transportation services adequate? What's the ferry schedule? Where's the nearest airport? Are roads plowed promptly in winter?

OPPOSITE: Borrowing architectural cues from the neighborhood helped this new home fit right in. **ABOVE:** The living room's focus is the board-and-batten fireplace.
RIGHT: The family room sofa bed and window seat provide sleep space for guests.

ABOVE: A soaring cathedral ceiling and dramatic fireplace make this home feel bigger.
RIGHT: Vintage-style drawer pulls and a display of favorite plates give the new kitchen cottage style.
OPPOSITE: The crow's-nest tower floods the interiors with natural light.

The Sullivans' 1,350-square-foot home has contemporary, open spaces, lots of light, and a subtle nautical theme inside, but architecturally, it settles in comfortably among this seaside town's bungalows. The neighborhood inspired the Sullivan home's multipane windows, hip roofs, and built-upon-itself feeling achieved with dormers, bump-out windows, and a crow's-nest tower. The combination of board-and-batten siding with shake shingles also fosters the illusion that the home evolved over time.

The couple shares these tips for building in an older neighborhood:

First, consult local planning groups before you design—or even before you make an offer on a site if you're concerned your dream home won't fit the area. This will save you time and money, and avoid disappointment. (The Sullivans' primary contact was the city planner, who presents home plans to architectural review boards, neighborhood associations, and historic committees.)

Second, pick an architect who is experienced in working with planning boards. Clarify how your architect charges for those dealings. (If you don't have an architect, count on spending time satisfying planning groups with drawings and information.)

Third, be patient with the approval process, and ask planning groups for a realistic time frame for each phase.

Finally, get all guidelines in writing to clarify direction and provide backup if an organization later disputes finished plans.

smaller AND SMARTER

Clearing the price-tag hurdle to turn your second-home dream into reality may be easier than you think. Now at home in the woods near Mt. Hood, Oregon, Nancy and Dennis Biasi used vision, determination, and do-it-yourself skills to stretch their budget and build their getaway for $60,000. The wooded lot with southern exposure and a river view was a bargain but cluttered with debris from a burned-out cabin. In the cleanup process, they unearthed a solid foundation and recycled it for their 1,200-square-foot home with an open floor plan, spectacular windows, and rustic character.

LEFT: Keeping the family room open and vaulting the ceiling to the rafters make this small home feel spacious. White walls provide airiness while also showcasing the beauty of the wood ceilings and window trim. **ABOVE:** Using standard units instead of custom-built windows on the back facade cuts costs, not the views. Dormers bring the light and woodsy vistas into the second floor. **OPPOSITE:** The rustic kitchen has secondhand appliances and a farm table that the family handcrafted with salvaged wood. Suspended from the ceiling, vintage lights play up the home's cottage style while flooding the kitchen with ambient light, even on rainy days.

THE PROACTIVE SEARCH

Even if you've done your homework and found your dream location, finding the right home or building site isn't always easy. Here are some tips.

▣ Beat the streets. Devote vacations and weekends to house hunting in person. Meet your would-be neighbors and get the word out that you're in the market.

▣ Shop the Internet. From small-town chambers of commerce and state tourism boards to national real estate companies, government agencies, and banks, it seems everybody has a website with information on everything, including evaluating locations worldwide, homes and land for sale, and financial options. Some include photos, the homes' vital statistics, and sales contacts.

▣ Make use of the newspapers in your "new" hometown and area. Place "want to buy" advertisements, and check out the "for sale" classifieds.

▣ See a home you like? Call or visit to see if the owners are considering a sale.

▣ Shop off-season. You may find bargain properties and less buyer competition.

▣ Call an experienced real estate agent who can advise you about available properties, preferred locations, and prices.

The Biasi family factored ideas from books and magazines into their design. To save space, they included double-duty features such as a guest room/den, storage and seating around the fireplace, and a kitchen table that doubles for work and dining.

They also used several budget-stretching strategies. By clearing the site themselves and finishing the home in phases, they could afford professional framing, plumbing, and custom kitchen cabinets. Building on the existing foundation and using stock windows also saved money. They shopped sales, salvage firms, damaged-freight companies, and the "building materials" want ads. Dennis bartered his graphic design and advertising services for tile from a local manufacturer. Wiring, tile installation, painting, and staining were family projects.

LEFT: Sleeping loft cabinetry is made from old wood; a sink adds convenience.
ABOVE: The couple's sons—Simon, left, and Chris—enjoy the river site.
OPPOSITE: Windowed dormers bring sunlight and views into the sleeping loft.

MIGRATORY PATTERNS

Where you buy depends in part on your personal migratory instincts. How much back-and-forth travel are you comfortable with? After a busy workweek, do you see yourself unwinding regularly in a weekend oasis within easy driving distance for your family and friends? Or, do you favor seasonal migration? If you plan to use a cottage as a summerlong family retreat or only occasionally for long vacations, distance may not be a consideration. Factor in all of these possibilities when you shop for square footage and a flexible floor plan with, for example, that extra bedroom to serve as a home office and sleep space for the inevitable guests. Because Woody Stover works out of a home office, his wife, Betsy, and their children enjoy the luxury of moving—every summer—into this lush lakeside retreat in northern Michigan.

RIGHT: This northern Michigan lake home is the family's full-time summer home and a weekend destination the rest of the year. **ABOVE:** A huge stone fireplace, hewn-log coffee table, and rustic log seating give the living room a put-up-your-feet feeling.

The Stovers and their four children had multiple roles in mind for the spacious two-story home—christened "Revels"—that they bought on Walloon Lake near Petoskey, Michigan, and remodeled to fit their needs. Although those rockers on the porch are inviting, Woody heads for his home office, once a sitting room, where he works while watching the children at play and Betsy tending her flower and vegetable gardens.

To make the home more gracious for entertaining and to expand the lake views, the Stovers incorporated an old porch when they enlarged the living room. A bigger foyer welcomes with seating space and room for guests to stash beach gear and bags. New skylights, a wall of windows, and French doors in the dining room keep the light and views flowing.

It's not just summer that finds the Stovers in residence. They head up for fall weekends so Betsy can harvest the last of her tomatoes and for Christmas. Whether it's the family or a crowd on hand, the home's casual attitude—with playful folk art, warm colors, and log seating plumped with comfy cushions—is an instant relaxer.

ABOVE: A gentle path leads to a generous dock—the perfect takeoff spot for a jump in the lake. Red Adirondack chairs add bright contrast to the woodsy setting.
RIGHT: Woody and son, Upton, share a lazy moment in the hammock.
OPPOSITE: The interior's bright colors spill onto rockers and a table on the porch.

The home's furnishings evolved over the years as the Stovers added family pieces, antiques, and locally handmade furniture. They mix it all against walls paneled in porchy beadboard and topped with heavy crown moldings. Quilts, country ticking, and old-fashioned floral fabrics play a fresh-and-light foil to chunky log pieces, such as the master suite's bed and the living room seating.

The Stovers envisioned a place where they could find solitude and also enjoy memory-making togetherness as a family. There's a hammock for reading beneath the trees, a picnic table for outside dining, and seating where the action is on the dock and the back porch.

BEFORE YOU BUY

You're ready to buy your dream home, but wait. Here are some things to consider before you sign:

▓ Take a deep breath. Are there any unpleasant agricultural or industrial smells? How about odors from septic tanks?

▓ Ask the neighbors if they are satisfied with the area. Where do they go for fun, shopping, recreation, or dinner out?

▓ Be realistic about your dreams. Identify immediate and long-term remodeling changes you would need to make in the home you are considering. Then figure out if it's doable on your budget.

▓ Research hidden costs. You may need flood insurance even if you're not on the water. Will you need to hire a property manager to keep an eye on things?

▓ Think bottom line. You may plan to stay forever, but what's the resale potential? Is this a summers-only spot, or do people also buy homes for year-round living?

▓ Protect your rights. For complex, long-distance deals and "by owner" sales, consider retaining a lawyer.

LEFT: An old bench with fresh cushions turns the foyer into a cozy spot for greetings and good-byes. **OPPOSITE:** Plump pillows and favorite quilts add color and softness to the master bedroom's rough-hewn four-poster.

IN TUNE WITH ITS site

LEFT: Framed by a large water oak and a grove of pecan trees, this new marshland cottage is raised more than 10 feet so floodwaters cannot reach living spaces. **OPPOSITE:** In this one-room cottage, the seating arrangement defines the boundary between the living area and the bedroom. French doors give the combined space access to the screen porch.

Just as you joyfully put down roots in a getaway spot you love, the home you build or remodel there can settle in, too, if it speaks the area's architectural vernacular.

When Becky Hollingsworth planned her ocean-view cottage near Charleston, South Carolina, she photographed old stables and garden houses and borrowed details for her own piece of history, a 600-square-foot home that resembles work buildings on local plantations. Tin roofs, elevated designs that protect homes from floodwaters, and hurricane shutters are typical in her Low-Country neighborhood. Grand plantations inspired the exterior's brick facing. The gable has a hayloft-style pulley; the fireplace is finished in indigenous oyster shells and mortar.

Full-height walls would have chopped up the interior of her petite retreat, so Becky designed it as an "everything room"—an open floor plan with partial walls defining spaces. The bedroom and living room share space so Becky always has a view of the fireplace.

Preserving the site's aged trees was a priority, so plenty of windows were needed for light and wraparound views. Vertical windows topped with half-round windows repeat through the home, and a single half-round window tucks under the front gable. White board-and-batten walls and natural finishes on the cypress ceiling and heart-pine floor make it even airier.

The open plan has definite advantages. Becky can snuggle into her bed and still enjoy a warming fire in the hearth on the opposite wall. Two comfortably overstuffed chairs mark the living room boundary. Storage is handled by a closet built into the partial wall and a new Scandinavian armoire designed specifically for easy installation and disassembly in smaller homes.

The compact L-shape kitchen downscaled appliance size but not efficiency. There's a small refrigerator and, instead of a traditional range, a microwave/convection oven. Overhead racks and cabinet tops store pots and crocks. A 10x20-foot screen porch is a traditional Southern amenity and adds flexible room for entertaining, relaxing, and sleep space for overnighters.

ABOVE: Collectibles infuse the living room with personality, and furnishings—chairs and an oversize ottoman—are simply all that's needed for comfort. **OPPOSITE:** Vaulting the ceiling on the old-fashioned screen porch that runs the width of the home makes it feel more spacious.

MAKE IT ENVIRONMENTALLY FRIENDLY

Water-rights issues and air and water quality can make or break a vacation location's appeal:

▩ Check drinking water quality with the local utility. City and county environmental management departments monitor lakes and creeks, but may check manmade lakes only if problems are reported.

▩ Know your property's water rights. For example, in Colorado, water rights don't come with the land and may need adjudication before closing, and in some places, private wells can't be drilled into known aquifers.

▩ Local environmental and health agencies can provide data on air pollution and pollens and other allergens.

A SENSE OF PLace

For second-home shoppers today, getting back to nature doesn't include tents or living off the land. Although they come ready to build or buy and tote microwaves and televisions along, falling in step with nature's rhythms is still the powerful draw. Just as an old house yields historic clues for restoration, there's design inspiration in the woods, at the beach, or in the mountains to make your second home look and feel, well, indigenous.

Kathleen and Dave Daniels gleaned ideas from the forest and lakes to link their new retreat near Orono, Minnesota, to the land. Wild rice, harvested locally, is the home's signature motif, with a stalk design cut into the stairway's balusters. Rock and wood were natural building materials because the home nestles among maple and oak trees on the edge of wetlands.

ABOVE: With a screen porch, steep snow-shedding roof, and stone chimney, this Minnesota home reprises the traditional design of north-woods cabins. **RIGHT:** Sized to match the scale of the great-room, the fieldstone fireplace brings intimacy and emotional warmth to the conversation area. **OPPOSITE:** An island, with a two-seater breakfast bar, defines the kitchen's work triangle and sets it apart from the dining area. The spice-hued cabinetry is topped with easy-care laminate countertops.

For their 1,792-square-foot home, the couple used cherry highlights on the maple floors, stairwell, and window trim. The living room hearth is constructed of locally quarried fieldstone. They took some cues from area architecture, steeply pitching the home's roof to shed snow easily and adding a rustic 12x12-foot screen porch that outsmarts mosquitoes and serves as the everyday family room.

Simple, casual, and comfortably down to earth is the Daniels' design style. So they borrowed another traditional idea—one-room living—from old north-woods cabins and translated it into an open-plan great-room that suits their easygoing, informal way of living and entertaining. Combining the living room, kitchen, and dining area under a dramatically vaulted ceiling also makes this modestly sized home seem roomier. The kitchen island defines the compact kitchen and also serves up buffet space.

Colors and textures keep things relaxed in the living room, where seating, upholstered in neutral fabrics, pairs up with an old wicker chair and vintage wood pieces that can take a few new scrapes and still look pretty. With an abundance of natural wood from floor to ceiling, white painted walls add to the light-and-airy mood.

LEFT: Stairway balusters have stylized cutouts of the stalks of wild rice, harvested from the region's waters. **ABOVE RIGHT:** Wicker chairs flank an old washstand on the porch, which is open to the rafters for a great outdoors feeling.

KNOW THE CLIMATE

Compiling data on temperatures, sunny days, rainfall, and storms can give you an idea of what living in your chosen area will be like.

◙ The National Oceanic and Atmospheric Administration (NOAA) offers a wealth of climate information on specific cities. Also check a region's climate data with the local environmental management agency, tourist board, and state climatologist's office.

◙ What's hot? "Average" temperatures don't tell the whole story, so look at daily temperatures throughout the year.

◙ It's not the heat, it's the humidity. Sun sounds great on snowy days, but how much heat and humidity is comfortable? People with respiratory problems may fare better in the drier Southwest than in humid Florida.

◙ Check local environmental departments for information on microclimates created by topography or prevailing winds.

◙ Local planners and emergency-response offices have maps of flood-prone areas and evacuation routes and preparedness tips for weathering tornadoes and hurricanes.

start from
scratch

Y ou found paradise—a mountainside acre,

a sliver of beach frontage, a patch of

woods—and now it's time to start

designing and building your retreat. As you tour the

following homes, take a cue from the owners who didn't

let setbacks, site restrictions, height limits, or less-than-

grand space diminish their visions of the ideal getaway.

Do panoramic views, outdoor living areas, and inviting

interiors for family fun and entertaining, plus guest

quarters, top your wish list? You can have it all with

ingenious home designs that turn dreams into reality.

RIGHT: Barely 20 feet wide, Corky and Pete Campbell's new, tri-level cottage on Seattle's Salmon Bay Waterway is a boat-watcher's paradise with windows and decks focused on the nautical parade.

A Narrow ESCAPE

In the shifting sands of tough building codes and vanishing waterfront property, finding one small footprint can be the key to building your dream retreat. Like kids with crayons, stay neatly within the lines. If a site has an existing structure and you build on that footprint, your plan may qualify as a renovation and win City Hall's approval more easily. Some areas also require incorporating an existing foundation or framing into new construction. That's the strategy Corky and Pete Campbell used to build their new cottage on Seattle's Salmon Bay Waterway. New houses on new pilings are not allowed, but setting the home on the existing pilings of an old fishnet drying shack qualified it as a fix-up project.

ABOVE: Seating in the midlevel living room focuses on water-view windows and a fireplace set into one wall. A banquette adds seating in a slice of space.
OPPOSITE: Deck access and overhead planks give the dining spot its nautical flavor.

Even the old shed's small footprint—20x36 feet—didn't stop the Campbells from planning a new 1,500-square-foot home clad in Maine-style shingles. They went vertical, stacking living spaces above the walkout-level master bedroom, and topping it off with a crow's-nest den/guest room. A gracious entry hall efficiently directs traffic to the stairs on one side, the kitchen on the other, and the living room straight ahead. As Charlie Vos, the project architect, says, the place "has a leave-the-world-behind quality. You're mesmerized by the boat traffic."

The open plan allows living areas to share views, light, and space. A trim kitchen opens to the living room across a peninsula that offers extra eating space.

OPPOSITE: The entry hall cuts between kitchen and bath into the living-dining room with a built-in rolltop desk. **ABOVE:** A wide entry boardwalk adds to the cottage's seaside ambience. A small gable dormer raises the spirit of the front door. **ABOVE RIGHT:** White paint and a plank ceiling put the kitchen in step with living areas.

SMALL SPACES THAT LIVE BIG

To make small homes shipshape, as the Campbells did, every inch of space and every design detail must work hard.

- Go high and light. White walls, a vaulted ceiling, large windows, and a see-through, open-tread stairway expand the visual space.
- Build in efficiency. Window seats and desks create purposeful niches and storage. A clever queen-size trundle bed can slide away like a drawer into low attic space, adding a guest room option to this den/office.
- Windows work. Abundant windows make small interiors airier. In tight waterfront spots like this, add privacy by minimizing side windows.

Open, airy, and bright were the Campbells' objectives for the home, so they used neutral hues and natural woods, with a dash of color and pattern in carpets, to create a serene mood. The living room fireplace was set into the waterside window wall to complement, not compete with, the view. Their architect, who is also a sailor, gave the home a fitting nautical theme. He made it as efficient as a boat's cabin with built-in furnishings from the fireside settees and a clever rolltop desk to the master suite's bed.

It was the romance of the sea that convinced the couple to build on the site. So they made certain that main-level gathering spots, such as the dining and living rooms, and private spaces, such as the master bedroom and den/guest room, frame the views with strategically placed windows and decks on three levels. Interior spaces flow beyond their boundaries to outdoor decks, making the home feel larger.

"We would have added more deck space, but I don't know that we would have added any rooms," Corky says.

Tucking the master suite below decks on the lower level affords the couple more privacy without compromising any amenities. The window-wrapped whirlpool tub bubbles only a few feet above high tide, and the Campbells launch rowboats off the suite's deck for morning exercise.

OPPOSITE: With a deck for relaxing and a desk for work, the lofty den doubles as Pete's office and a guest room with a stowaway bed.
ABOVE: Even the master suite's built-in bed, with storage below, has a waterway view through French doors to a deck.
RIGHT: A low-perimeter wall shields whirlpool tub bathers without blocking the view.

LITTLE LUXURIES

OPPOSITE: The home's back follows the sun with an array of south-facing windows. **LEFT:** Glass blocks frame a fixed pane in the living room's "light box" bay. **BELOW:** The cherry mantel naturally contrasts with more finished materials, and a horizontal trellis accents the ceiling.

As you tinker with square footage, floor plans, and amenities for your getaway home, ask yourself: Do I need this feature? This space? Will it enhance my quality of life? Minneapolis architect Sarah Susanka says that building a home that satisfies your personal expectations and needs has more to do with the quality of the design and details than with the square footage itself. She embraced that philosophy in designing a 2,440-square-foot home for herself and her architect husband, Jim Larson. Smart site orientation and thoughtful window placement capture views of woods and lowlands, and multifunctional living areas keep the home's size down so upscale architectural elements and details fit the budget.

Panelized construction enabled the couple to get the custom home up fast before winter set in. It took just a few days to assemble the factory-made panels for the walls, floors, and roof on the foundation.

Sarah heightened interest in the combined living/dining/kitchen space by varying ceiling heights, creating nooks for reading, and adding nighttime drama with recessed lights that cast light and shadow through the wooden ceiling trellises.

OPPOSITE: Bookshelves put potentially wasted landing space to work. Near the foot of the stairs, a book nook includes a window seat for reading and lounging. **LEFT:** Dining, living, and kitchen areas share space and light. **ABOVE:** The furniture-look kitchen cabinets have elegant black accents.

By deleting such things as a separate dining room and extra bathrooms, the couple could afford custom woodwork, convenient lighting control systems, wood floors, quality cabinetry, decorative tile, and other custom features that make everyday living a pleasure. Throughout the home, contemporary comfortable furnishings in neutral hues showcase the woodwork and Oriental rugs layered over carpet.

OPPOSITE: When mosquitoes invade the deck, the screen porch makes a relaxing refuge. **ABOVE:** Sarah and Jim stroll through the backyard that they left as natural as possible. **RIGHT:** Attic ambience makes the top-floor master bedroom a great getaway. A roof window lights a snug reading corner.

COASTING HOME

After a day at your own backyard beach, you relax on your deck while watching a cascade of ocean breakers. Sound good? Despite stringent building codes and the potential for storm damage and erosion, waterfront properties remain in high demand. If you buy with care, keeping the area's weather and geology in mind, you can have your ocean view and a new home, too, by outfitting it to withstand the elements.

Leighton and Karin McIlvaine wisely battened down the hatches on their dramatic Maine cliffhanger that replaced a summer home Leighton's grandfather built there in the 1920s. They topped the 1,400-square-foot retreat with a cupola—an enclosed version of a widow's walk—for a high view over offshore islands. Like the rest of the sturdy home, the aerie is wrapped in insulated windows. "We've been up there in extremely bad storms, and it's still tight and feels solid," Leighton says.

RIGHT: This summer home was designed to look as if wind and water had sheared it clean. **ABOVE:** The 8x12-foot cupola offers built-in seating, a solid oak floor, and some of the best views around.

Recalling how everyone loved the old home's ocean-view porch, the McIlvaines gave the new living room the same view— but better because now they can relax and enjoy the scene, rain or shine. A screen porch and deck are fair-weather retreats. Large windows treated with honeycomb shades for extra insulation give every room a view. Cedar siding was brushed with preservative and stain, then left to weather.

ABOVE: Meals for a crowd are easy in the efficient kitchen. **RIGHT:** The master bedroom occupies the entire second floor. **FAR RIGHT:** The living room's gently curved windows reach out to capture the view. The fireplace takes the chill away on cool Maine days.

STYLE ON A SHOESTRING

Your lake lot was a rare find, and you envision living big. But the numbers are working against you. Once you subtract for erosion setbacks and zoning regulations, you may be left with the incredible shrinking footprint. That was the dilemma these Lake Michigan homeowners faced. A dune blocked the lake view and, minus setbacks, their 50-foot-wide lot left little room to maneuver.

With a creative home design, architect John Allegretti made the math literally add up because up was the only way to go. The 2,107-square-foot weekend home elevates the open-plan family room, dining area, kitchen, and the master suite to the middle level for optimum views over that pesky dune. The lower level has guest and media rooms, and the top floor has family bedrooms. The owners told their architect: Make comfort and function the priorities, forget frills, and stick to a $200,000 budget.

OPPOSITE: This Lake Michigan cottage dips into nature's paint box for the exterior's water, sky, and sand hues. **ABOVE:** The family room gathers new upholstered seating and antiques around the porcelain-tiled fireplace.

ABOVE: Down-to-earth colors—a sage green picture rail and sand-hued walls—ground the dining area with its cathedral ceiling and upstairs overlook. **ABOVE RIGHT:** The glassed-in gable draws light and views into the balcony and bedrooms. **OPPOSITE:** The home's lake side is loaded with windows. White porch-style rails give cottage charm to a deck that invites relaxing.

BEAUTY AND THE BASICS

What's on your wish list for a weekend home? If your plan covers the basics, your family will enjoy it more.

▣ Is it comfortable? Furniture groupings divide this family room into cozy gathering spots, and the backdrop colors make it easy to mix new and old pieces.

▣ How does it function? Here, the deck is big enough for dining, entertaining, and lounging. Bedrooms spread over three levels offer privacy.

▣ Does space feel tight? Open up rear walls with glass, glass, and more glass, or add a bay window to bring in more sights, light, and a feeling of space. Glass-front cabinets and mirrored backsplashes can open up any kitchen.

▣ Is it easy care? Flooring of level-loop carpet, tile, laminates, or polyurethaned hardwoods handle heavy use.

The symmetrical home with wide overhangs is reminiscent of Craftsman-style architecture, and the bright palette takes its cue from older, colorful cottages on the lake. To keep things light inside, Allegretti created a "transparent" stairway, with spindles and open risers instead of walls, at the home's core. In the vaulted family room, he filled the high-rise gable end with divided-light windows. The family room is the heart of the home, and a railed overlook connects it to the upper level. "We tried to create an intimate niche for fireplace seating," he says. To make the most of the small home, walls work hard with built-ins and dimmable sconce lighting. Green on the picture rail and trim forges a color and architectural link throughout.

OPPOSITE: Opening off the stairway, the upper levels' small decks capture light and breezes. **ABOVE LEFT:** Floor-to-ceiling bedroom built-ins add more storage than standard furniture. **ABOVE:** A trim vanity, white walls, and a transom window visually expand the bath.

LOGGING ON

The luxury and convenience packed into modern log homes have prompted an outbreak of cabin fever. A descendant of the humble homesteads that nurtured Abe Lincoln and tamed the frontier, log homes can be built fast and customized to include open floor plans, large view windows, and as much square footage as your family needs in a getaway home. Architecturally, they're a natural choice for mountain and wooded sites such as Harry and Lynne McNamara's 2 acres backing up to a national forest near Aspen, Colorado. To tone down the rusticity and open up light-filled spaces in their custom log home, they chose a honey hue for exposed logs and put textured drywall, instead of more typical tongue-and-groove paneling, on some walls and between ceiling beams. Four bedrooms, plus a 20x15-foot living room that opens to a dining area and kitchen, create the "social home" the couple wanted for entertaining their three grown children, extended family, and friends.

FAR LEFT: A great-room window captures mountain views. **NEAR LEFT:** The staircase features a bark-clad newel post.
BELOW: Gables add a look of cozy charm.

From idea to finished landscaping, designing and building a custom log home may take 12 to 18 months, but once the foundation and subfloor are in place and the log trucks arrive, the pace picks up. The McNamaras' home was assembled in under 4 days.

Furnishings with the character and comfort of age fit the home's informal personality, so the couple scoured auctions and salvage shops for such items as door hardware, light fixtures, and doors for the hand-built stone fireplace. To break up the all-wood backdrops, they painted some furniture and combined painted and natural finishes in kitchen cabinetry.

OPPOSITE: A light-finish table, reupholstered chairs, and casual valances relax the dining area. **ABOVE:** A butcher-block island expands the country kitchen's food-prep space. **RIGHT:** The breakfast bar's brass rail came from a secondhand shop.

BUILDING THE AMERICAN CLASSIC

Log homes come as predesigned kits or more-expensive custom versions. Here are tips on selecting a manufacturer:

▣ Dealer or factory-direct? Factory-direct may be cheaper, but working through a local dealer often is easier.

▣ Up to code? Some log home companies employ architects who check your site's seismic activity, snow loads, and frost dip to upgrade their standard plans.

▣ What's in a package? A plan and building materials only, or are windows, doors, subfloor framing, and decking included? Does the company provide technical support while you build?

▣ Do it yourself? Some companies offer training camps.

▣ Check the warranty. It may cover log replacement, not labor.

ABOVE: The master bath doubles up on function with twin sinks that are set into natural-finish cabinetry highlighted with green trim. **RIGHT:** Country-fresh furnishings and vintage quilts from Lynne's collection maintain the master bedroom's clean and cozy look. The couple turned dead aspen branches into curtain rods, and Harry handcrafted the armoire for extra storage.

GOING MODULAr

With modular or panelized-shell construction, you can put your cottage plans on fast forward. But what if you want a custom, architect-designed home? No problem. Most major home manufacturers can prefabricate custom designs. Architect Wayne Neale and his wife, Sherri, chose modular construction for their 2,000-square-foot cottage in Rehoboth Beach, Delaware, for economy and because they live too far away to supervise lengthy site-built construction. Based on Wayne's plans, a company prefabricated the home in two sections, including the porch, most of the plumbing, wiring, cabinets, and carpet. A shingled exterior, Cape Cod-style roof, and porch help the home blend with its old-time neighbors. To meet a $70,000 budget, they kept bedrooms spare and the kitchen small. A French-door connection to the porch opens the living/dining room to the outdoors.

OPPOSITE: Double-decker porches and graceful columns give this charming beach cottage streetside appeal. Wide front steps and double screen doors create the old-fashioned feeling associated with Victorian porches. **ABOVE RIGHT:** A front screen porch with Adirondack chairs seems almost a requisite for casual summertime relaxation. **RIGHT:** A New England home inspired the upper-level veranda's cedar-clad, barrel-vault ceiling.

BEACH HOUSE IN A BOX

If you are considering fast, cost-effective modular construction:

■ Check out the company. Interview at least three firms registered with the Modular Building Systems Council of the National Association of Home Builders before selecting one.

■ Check builders' references and view their modular home projects.

■ Be patient. Waits vary from 45 days to 8 months for delivery.

■ Personalize it. Most modular home companies have staff architects who use computerized drawings to assist you in making changes.

ABOVE and OPPOSITE: A counter separates the kitchen and living/dining room. A fireplace and built-ins create a snug focal point. **RIGHT:** Money-saving stock cabinets sport a pickled finish.

ISLAND TIMBERFRAME

On the road to paradise, traffic jams are inevitable, especially if you're heading to the shore. If you're lucky, you could end up sailing away, not driving, to your weekend home. When it's getaway time, Scott and Christina Koons Baker and family hop a ferry to Orcas Island, north of Seattle, where their new, timberframe bungalow overlooks manmade Eagle Lake.

The couple purchased one of the development's 53 circular lots, all 100 feet in diameter. The design guidelines encourage Craftsman-style homes, limit footprints to 2,499 square feet, and heights to 33 feet. A timberframe systems supplier engineered the home based on the couple's open floor plan and delivered it as a precut package.

OPPOSITE and RIGHT: The great-room includes a window seat/guest bed with bonus storage below. **ABOVE and RIGHT:** The home's exposed structure also is decorative.

Precut home systems are often easier to build on hard-to-access sites. Here, the precut package included this home's frame, windows, fasteners, insulation, roof, and paneling. Critical to post-and-beam construction is a level and square subfloor. "We use laser equipment to check along the way," builder Don Wallis explains. "A timberframe home is not forgiving to anything out of square by much more than an eighth of an inch." Christina designed the home for one-story living with the great-room, master bedroom, and laundry on the main level.

LEFT: An eating bar faces the great-room, offering a convenient spot for snacks and chatting with the cook. **TOP:** The dock is great for lakeside picnics and relaxing. **ABOVE:** Painted kitchen cabinetry complements and contrasts with the home's abundant woods.

ABOVE The vanity echoes the kitchen's green accents. **ABOVE RIGHT:** The master suite is compact but comfortable with built-ins for books. **OPPOSITE:** A deck off the great-room and kitchen takes in nature's vistas. Acrylic fabrics are moisture- and sun-resistant.

The vaulted ceiling makes the main level feel more spacious, and for year-round warmth, there are a wood-burning stove and, beneath the pine floors, a radiant heat system. Against the rustic backdrop, colorful rugs and pillows spice up an easygoing mix of overstuffed and painted furnishings. In this 2,300-square-foot retreat, Christina devoted the lower level to a guest suite and playroom, and the third level to the children's bedroom, bath, and sleeping loft. The home took eight months to complete.

PERSONALITY IN DETAIL

Shop wisely and you may find the perfect architect-designed home plan in books or online—one with view windows galore, plenty of family-friendly spaces, outdoor living areas, and guest quarters. If the stock plan you choose is as classic, clean-line, and adaptable as the one, *opposite*, from Archway Press, you can make simple exterior changes to help it reflect your style or or that of your region. Perhaps the plan's vertical siding and casement windows aren't rustic enough for your mountain site, or maybe you'd like to add some cottage charm with a porch and deck railing of turned balusters. By substituting siding materials, trims, window styles, and other design elements, you can give a basic exterior a different personality.

For starters, take a look at existing homes in your area so you can put your cottage in harmony with the neighborhood. Are most of the homes in your coastal setting Victorian in spirit, or do they reflect the spare look of classic modern designs? Would a rugged stone chimney and log-look cedar siding make your home more at home in the woods? Is stucco a better fit for your Sunbelt retreat than clapboards? Once you've checked out the neighbors, check out an architecture book or two from the library. By acquainting yourself with materials common to classic home designs, you can coax a basic plan into making a strong design statement.

A CHANGE OF PLANS

Most home-plan companies will, for a fee, customize a floor plan, add a garage, or offer alternative ideas for exterior embellishments. As you plan, consider these changes you can make to standard plans.

▪ Add a walkout basement. If your lot slopes to the rear or the side, it could add affordable living space. If the backyard has prime views, it makes even more sense to bring that view into the basement level.

▪ No pane, no gain. Use bay windows or replace standard windows with French doors to link indoors and out.

▪ Live outdoors. Add a wraparound deck or a screen porch so interiors live like the great outdoors.

▪ Flip the plan end for end. It could help your home take advantage of views, sunlight, and the terrain. Many plans can be ordered in a reverse format to aid builders in making changes.

▪ Add a garage, or move the garage if it blocks the view. Relocate a tuck-under garage if you don't like trekking up steps with groceries.

▪ Plan ahead. Buy a reproducible plan set because blueprints have copyright protection, making it illegal to copy most plans.

OPPOSITE, TOP LEFT: The *original design*, a 32x32-foot square, offers simple, bold lines that, depending on your choice of materials and details, can assume many identities. The overhanging eaves and braces make especially good starting points for a Chalet-style or Victorian change of face.

OPPOSITE, TOP RIGHT: Sculpted fascia boards, shutters and railings with decorative cutouts, and exposed rafters on the overhangs lend *chalet* style. Picket-fence-style vertical siding overlaps horizontal siding to hint at the decorated wood exteriors associated with chalets.

OPPOSITE, BOTTOM LEFT: To give the same plan clean-lined *minimalist modern* style, remove the overhangs and use vertical, grooved plywood siding—even on the chimney.

OPPOSITE, BOTTOM RIGHT: As if detailed by a country craftsman in the mid- to late 1800s, this version makes a nod to *Victorian* Stick and Carpenter Gothic styles with board-and-batten siding, the gable's decorative truss, pediments to elongate the windows, and a spirelike pinnacle over the main gable. Criss-cross railings repeat the form of the diagonal wood detailing often applied to Stick-style homes.

Architect: Roger Taylor Panek, AIA. Home plan #2129, courtesy Archway Press, Inc., at www.archwaypress.com. Illustrations: Lewis Bryden.

ORIGINAL EXTERIOR

CHALET VARIATION

MINIMALIST MODERN VARIATION

VICTORIAN VARIATION

FIX IT up

ocation, location, location is the real estate rule that applies to second-home shopping, too. Buying a less-than-perfect home in the perfect spot will get you as far as the beach, the lakeshore, or the mountains on weekends, but remodeling to suit your vision and lifestyle will take you all the way home to the getaway of your dreams. Adapt ideas from the homeowners in this chapter who added more of the good stuff—more views, light, comfort, outdoor living areas, and space. They tuned up landscapes to harmonize with nature, rebuilt character inside and out, and winterized for year-round fun.

RIGHT: An outdoor fireplace transforms a patio into an al fresco living room. This new hearth is built of river rock quarried near this Bainbridge Island, Washington, home. Handcrafted wooden checkers turn patio stones into a game board.

DEVELOPING A VISION

TOP: Built-ins frame mountain views. **ABOVE and OPPOSITE:** A new river-rock fireplace has a second flue for the outdoor hearth.

Decades of well-meaning fixes can blur any older home's character; a sensitive renovation, however, can bring its style back into focus. Dan Klaue used his love of rustic Arts and Crafts style to pull together his Bainbridge Island, Washington, home— a kit-built log cabin topped with a later, inappropriate addition. Dan lightened up spaces with new windows and established continuity by repeating elements, such as cedar ceilings. He also bumped out the living room 6 feet for a river-rock fireplace tucked into a traditional Arts and Crafts inglenook.

TOP and ABOVE: A pass-through and enlarged deck ease entertaining. **OPPOSITE:** A bay window lightens the dining room and provides extra

COLORING YOUR COTTAGE

Picking a palette for your cottage exterior? Use these tips.

▣ Experiment first. Take a black-and-white photo of your house, enlarge and copy it, then use color markers to try out a variety of paint color combinations.

▣ Play visual tricks. Dark colors make a house appear smaller; a coat of light paint adds an illusion of size.

▣ Simplify. Often, one body color, a lighter tint or darker shade of that hue on trim, and a dark sash are all you need.

▣ Consider historic colors. Made by several paint companies, such paints offer darker, richer, more mellow hues.

▣ Be a copycat. Repeat the colors you see on another home or a sample palette shown on a paint color chart.

preserving THE PAST

Reconnecting with the past and simpler times is, for many, the ideal antidote to today's fast-paced lifestyles. If idyllic weekends in the country sound appealing, roam the back roads and you may find an old farmstead to remodel into your ideal second home. When Paula and Peter Fasseus and their two children, Alexis and Drew, wanted a weekend change from high-rise life and commuting, they searched the rolling hills and dense woods along the border of Indiana and Michigan. To these city dwellers, the 1830 clapboard farmhouse they bought was a treasure, with its own barn, an apple orchard, and a peaceful pond on 15 acres. Remodeling, they insisted, couldn't change its charm. "This little farmhouse on the winding road gave us a sense of stepping back in time, when life was very simple," Paula says.

OPPOSITE: Weekend entertaining is frequently on the agenda in the new, two-story addition's family room that draws comfy seating around a fireplace flanked by built-ins for storage and display. **ABOVE:** Slipcovered seating, airy wicker, and mismatched tables imbue the home's original living room with fresh cottage charm.

There was no question that this active family that loves weekend entertaining needed more living space. Their challenge was to remodel, expand, and redecorate the 900-square-foot home while preserving its 19th-century ambience.

Although the two-story addition is obviously new, it echoes details of the original home. The family room has two tiers of old-fashioned, double-hung windows that capture views and don't need curtains. Walls are paneled in wide planks, nailed directly to the drywall and left uncaulked to look like barn siding. Bright white paint covers walls and woodwork to unify the architecture and create a clean backdrop for easygoing furnishings and collectibles, such as the family's rooster figurines inspired by real-life counterparts in the barnyard. Here, and in the kitchen, an aniline dye treatment gives new pine floorboards a mellow, aged look.

The farm's casual, drop-in lifestyle means unexpected dinner guests, so the new island kitchen opens to a dining area. An antique pine dining table is long enough to accommodate everybody. Glass doors in the simple white cabinets are reminiscent of old general stores, and the butcher-block counters of country meat cutters. One perk of country living? The herbs, tomatoes, and other fresh vegetables that go from garden to table.

ABOVE: A new multipane window offers a view of the garden, orchard, and pond. Geraniums and ivy bring the outdoors in. **RIGHT:** The original post-and-beam barn was remodeled with a dance floor for hoedowns. **OPPOSITE:** Paneling, butcher block, and handmade cabinets wrap the convenience of a commercial range and warming drawers in country style. The island mimics farm tables of the past.

OPPOSITE: A mudroom potting bench is handy for washing vegetables and arranging flowers. **LEFT:** This remodeled 1830 farmhouse kept its character. **BELOW:** The farm's menagerie includes chickens.

In the remodeling, the family encountered typical old-home problems, such as cracked plaster in the original bedrooms. After making sure the cracks weren't a structural red flag and doing repairs, they took the easy-does-it approach, covering walls with floral paper and ceilings with white-painted beadboard.

Following the road less traveled to their retreat agrees with the Fasseus family. After tending the garden, they bicycle tree-lined lanes together, relax in the porch swing or chairs by the pond, and take tea at a dressed-up garden table.

"It's like paradise," Peter says.

LEAVING WELL ENOUGH ALONE

You can have the best of both worlds—architectural character and light-filled, open living spaces—if a remodeling honors your home's history and style.

▣ Preserve with a pro. Pick an architect with expertise in preservation and renovation projects. Check local and state historical groups and schools of architecture for names.

▣ Save face. Keep the street facade intact. When possible, site an addition to the home's back, or back and to the side. Open up ceilings, delete walls, widen room-to-room openings, and combine spaces for contemporary living without disturbing the exterior.

▣ Pick building materials and colors similar to the original ones.

▣ Let the original roof pitch and the style and placement of windows be your guide as you plan room additions.

▣ Repeat details. Match exterior shutters and trims with old ones. Inside, carry matching moldings and hardwood floors into new additions.

WINTERIZING A summer HOME

Although a summer home is, by nature, a place to relax, there's no reason to let the calendar dictate how much time your family spends there. The need to renew your spirit doesn't stop when the temperatures drop. Hiking through fallen leaves and playing in the snow can be as much fun as reading and rocking on a breezy porch or barbecuing on the beach. Discovering that summer was just too short, Chicagoan Dennis Barnette decided to transform his 1,100-square-foot Michigan lake cottage into a year-round escape. In the process, he created what he describes as "a classic cottage that looks as if it's evolved over generations."

OPPOSITE: New French doors and casement windows make the living room addition the sunniest spot in the home, and the garden view inspired the floral fabrics and birdhouse accents.
ABOVE: The stove adds old-fashioned charm and keeps the space toasty on chilly days.
ABOVE RIGHT: Replacing former driveway space, a charming gate and brick sidewalk lead to a bright new gabled entry, complete with a welcoming front porch and a friendly red door.

LEFT: Minimal size gives the bumped-out breakfast nook its cozy charm. Perfect for solo coffee and bird-watching, the spot can seat six, thanks to a storage-packed built-in banquette.
OPPOSITE: The expansive garden offers lots of sitting spots, including this shady arbor that's enclosed on three sides with latticework for privacy and set with wicker chairs for relaxing and dining.

Dennis started the makeover with energy-efficient changes the summer-only cottage needed. Working with a carpenter, he added insulation, new windows, and a new furnace to replace old baseboard heaters. A vintage-style wood stove in the living room helps ward off the chill, too. But year-round livability involved more than just turning up the heat. There would be no outdoor grilling and patio entertaining in winter. So, he traded the cottage's galley for a new, larger kitchen with a bump-out dining nook and plenty of room for guests to join in the cooking. The new kitchen incorporated space from a spare bedroom, and the old kitchen became the pantry.

Because Dennis wanted to use the home throughout the year, a screen porch was enclosed for year-round use. A painted floor helps the space retain its seasonal charm.

"This is one of the few areas of the cottage that is really just for one—the perfect place to read a book on a quiet afternoon," he says.

Also enclosed, the original sleeping porch now serves as the snug master bedroom. In contrast to the room's small size, its fabulous four-poster offers generous comfort.

After he remodeled the house for four-season use, Dennis found that bright whites and summer casual furnishings can seem downright cold when the snow flies. Colorful rugs and fabrics, overstuffed seating, and mellow wood antiques banish the chill.

LEFT: Perennials and evergreen shrubs outline the brick-paver patio that has plenty of chairs and chaises for sunning and enjoying the garden. **OPPOSITE:** A custom-made farmhouse-style bed with high posts creates an island of comfort in any weather.

UPGRADE FOR YEAR-ROUND COMFORT

To make a fair-weather retreat just as comfortable in snowy January as it is in sunny July:

⊞ Beef up the insulation. In older homes built for summer-only use, it's probably inadequate or nonexistent.

⊞ Control the temperature. Install a furnace—and air conditioning if your climate demands it. If the floor plan has guest quarters in a self-contained wing, consider energy-efficient, zoned heating and cooling.

⊞ Add a secondary heat source—a fireplace or wood-burning stove for rainy, chilly days.

⊞ Dodge drafts. Caulk or weather-strip existing windows and doors. Replace old or single-pane windows with energy-efficient insulated glass.

⊞ Avoid frozen pipes. If you're using the home year-round, you may need to relocate some water lines and insulate pipes because you won't be draining lines for winter.

⊞ Wrap a screen porch in operable windows that create wintertime coziness *and* summertime breeziness.

⊞ Landscape with winter beauty in mind. Include evergreen trees and shrubs to keep garden views interesting with subtle color when the snow piles up.

⊞ Add convenience with more storage or a garage to ensure that your car starts on winter mornings.

BRINGING THE OUTSIDE IN

Whether your retreat overlooks dense woods, mountain peaks, or pounding surf, a remodeling that forges strong links to the outdoors can make it a natural wonder. Well-placed windows can erase the boundary between indoors and out if you opt for tall, to-the-floor glazing. Expansive windows open up wraparound vistas; smaller panes frame the landscape like art. Porches and decks stretch a home's livable footprint and cast nature as the backdrop. When Henry and Cheryl Kluck updated their 1913, two-room farmhouse in the Michigan woods, the result was part tree house and part modern loft that captures light and lets it flow.

Overlooking a tree-lined ravine and creek, the couple's home, with its mossy-green cedar siding and low horizontal roof pitch, almost disappears into the landscape for a look that's vaguely prairie style and definitely inviting. A screen porch entry offers glimpses of the interior through peekaboo windows. Inside, these avid collectors layered flea market finds, family mementos, and country-casual furnishings.

OPPOSITE: Tall double-hung windows link the living room to its wooded setting. High on the wall, a pair of transom windows adds barnlike character. The couple's serendipitous collections add more personality to the living room, where treasures line a window-hugging shelf, and an old quilt perks up the sofa. **ABOVE:** The cottage's front entry was relocated and enclosed with a screen porch to gain more outdoor living space.

Through a series of remodeling projects, the couple made certain the home retained its vintage flavor. When they bought the old home on a 1-acre site, it was structurally precarious. The foundation was iffy, the floor joists were 3 inches out of level, and the existing roof was unstable. They saved 14 feet of the south wall and 15 feet of the west wall. "The rest was thrown away," Henry says.

Although remodeling retained the home's footprint, the house lives bigger because of high-ceilinged, open-plan spaces. The couple added a new screen porch/entry with Adirondack furniture and a deck that zigzags around to preserve trees. More expensive true divided-light windows were a budget priority, but the Klucks saved money by installing vinyl flooring instead of hardwood.

Operable windows on one wall of the screen porch catch breezes for the great-room/kitchen. "The easiest thing was to make the room flow together," Cheryl says. "When we're entertaining, it works well. Guests can sit and chat at the bar/counter." The kitchen seems to float in the space, and glass panes in upper cabinets enhance the open feel. There's a view, too, through a window above the sink that looks through the foyer and porch. Even on rainy days, the great-room is bright with skylights and tall windows.

To soften the home's newness, the couple mixes rustic twig and painted pieces with country woods, cottage-style antiques, and in the living room, twin guest-ready sofa beds in neutral slipcovers.

OPPOSITE: The tile-topped island offers seating for casual meals and chatting with guests, and on the kitchen side, it steps down to a work counter. To keep the kitchen light, cabinet doors have glass insets, and the interior window above the sink catches light from foyer skylights. **ABOVE:** In the powder room, country-style beadboard wainscot underlines a collection of old hand mirrors in light-hued celluloid called French ivory. Cheryl and her father-in-law share a passion for collecting the vintage mirrors that were popular from the mid-1880s to the 1920s.

BEFORE YOU REMODEL

Ask the right questions to be sure your plans are on the right track.

▣ Is it worth it dollar-wise? Are your neighbors remodeling? Are homes selling fast? Ask an appraiser how your project may impact resale value.

▣ Can your project meet zoning, setback or height restrictions, or related ordinances? Are you affected by historic district regulations?

▣ Would small changes work instead of a major redo? Adding a porch, another bath, skylights, energy-efficient windows, dormers, or a deck offers a quick, less costly way to add livability.

ABOVE: Peekaboo windows create symmetry and ventilation on the new screen porch, paneled in knotty pine and set with simple, rustic furnishings.

OPPOSITE: A gridlike railing keeps views as open as possible on the deck, zigzagged to preserve precious trees.

ADDING A sunroom

To live bigger and better, sometimes a cottage doesn't need a whole-house remodeling. It just needs one glorious, multitalented room that reaches out and grabs the light and the view. Sunrooms do that and more. Taking cues from their remodeled post-and-beam barn-style home in Iowa, Ron and Denise Whitman worked with architect H. Ronald Walker to design a new sunroom shaped like the corncribs that dot the rural landscape. Separated from the house by a short hallway, a nearly freestanding room like this can be added onto various home types for dining, lounging—and even guest quarters if you include sleepable seating.

LEFT: Set on a wooded hillside above a river, the sunroom makes a four-season refuge with glider windows of insulated low-E glass. In warm weather, all the windows, top and bottom, slide open to create a virtual screen porch. Colorful rugs and cushions change with the seasons. **TOP:** Honeycomb shades on the front windows fend off sun, heat, and cold, rising from the sill up for privacy. **ABOVE:** A short hallway connects the barn house to its "corncrib" sunroom.

OPENING UP THE interiors

If your getaway has started to feel more cramped than cozy, easy architectural changes or a small, but well-planned, addition can make it live bigger and smarter.

What would enhance your life at your retreat—light-filled interiors, more sleep space, more storage, a big deck? Deleting walls, opening up ceilings, and adding French doors give interiors the illusion of more space and the reality of more light. Converting space under the roof is usually less costly than adding on.

Leighton and Karin McIlvaine incorporated all of the above in the redesign of "The Cat's Meow," their 11x18-foot guest cottage on Maine's rocky coast. They bumped out the floor plan with an 18x13-foot addition to add a larger kitchen with a loft bunk room that combines the feeling of camping out with all the comforts of home. They kept the pine-paneled backdrops, exposed ceiling beams, and floors light and natural to make the compact spaces seem roomier. Guests appreciate the new kitchen that allows self-sufficiency.

ABOVE: The main bedroom was once the whole structure, but the living area and tiny kitchen were relocated to an addition. Walls have random-width, pine paneling. Open beams on the sky-blue ceiling create architectural interest. **OPPOSITE:** This weekend guest cottage expanded its livability with an ocean-view deck and a loft bunk room in the new addition.

The success of any remodeling project comes down to construction, so picking an experienced, reputable contractor is important.

■ Ask the pros. Architects and designers have area contractors and finish carpenters they work with regularly, but you're not limited by their recommendations. Contact the local chapter of professional trade organizations, such as the National Association of the Remodeling Industry or the National Association of Home Builders.

■ Ask neighbors who have remodeled to recommend local contractors.

■ Request about 20 recent project references, especially any that are similar to the remodeling you plan, then contact at least six to learn how satisfied the owners are with the work.

■ Is the builder licensed, bonded, or registered as required locally and insured for liability and workers' compensation? Verify credentials with the state licensing board and check the Better Business Bureau for complaints.

With the addition of the loft bunk room that's accessible via ladder from the new living room/kitchen, the cottage now accommodates six guests. The built-in double bunks hug one wall of the loft, leaving floor space for wicker seating. There's no need for dressers because the bottom bunk has drawers beneath it. A new, wraparound deck with a hot tub expands the cottage's living space.

OPPOSITE: The compact kitchen is efficient for meals and snacks. A shaded deck lies just beyond the doors.
ABOVE: High-rise windows light the new loft, which includes built-in bunks, cozy seating, and storage.

WELCOMING GueSTS

OPPOSITE: Pillows and cushions in butter-soft fabrics invite guests to curl up and enjoy the view from this window seat in the bay. **LEFT:** The kitchen's cabinetry with brass hardware and raised panels blends with the backdrop and living room furnishings. **ABOVE:** With new bay windows, French doors, and easygoing furnishings, this old stable is now an airy guest retreat. It's just a short walk across the patio to the main house.

L iving even part-time in a fabulous vacation spot will make you especially popular, so count on occasional weekend guests to share walks in the woods, water sports, or family-style feasts. Where do you find extra space for guests? Attics, porches, or walk-out basements could be converted easily. Add a privacy screen, and a sitting loft can house company. Or consider the property's outbuildings, as Bill and Linda Casey did when they needed to round up guest quarters at their Arizona home. With space-saving techniques, they transformed an old stable into a charming, one-bedroom cottage. To capture light, expand the interior space, and break up the stable's flat exterior, they installed big bay windows in the living room/kitchen and the bedroom. Although the bumped-out bays added minimal square footage, it was enough for built-in drawer storage and window seating.

Charming cottage furnishings and fabrics in pale yellow, desert brown, and rosy terra-cotta hues create cozy comfort. For convenience, one wall of the main room is a compact kitchen with a microwave oven so guests feel self-sufficient from morning coffee through late-night snacks. White open-beam ceilings and light window treatments make the small space airier. Essentials, such as the graceful metal bed and sconce lighting, do the job without gobbling up floor space.

ABOVE: A built-in chest of drawers gives guests a spot to stow their stuff. **OPPOSITE:** For a serene and restful mood, the bedroom limits color, pattern, and furnishings to a pretty and comfortable few.

FACELIFTING THE exterior

OPPOSITE: Half-log siding turned this once-nondescript ranch into a rustic cabin that snuggles into its wooded site. **LEFT:** Awnings shade the screen porch accented with birch-log trim and a collection of rustic seating and ethnic blankets. **ABOVE:** An old totem pole watches over the patio, where Adirondack chairs gather around a man-made pond.

If you think a rustic lodge deep in the forest would make the perfect escape from hectic city life, Stanley Paul would agree. He, too, is enchanted by the rugged romance of early 20th-century camps, cabins, and Adirondack lodges. This faceless 1950s ranch didn't fit his vacation-home ideal or the rugged, wooded site near Lake Michigan when he bought it, but Stanley soon changed all that. First came a cabin-style facelift with log-look siding, inside and out. Outside, the builder stripped away aluminum siding and applied the half-logs over exterior sheathing. The half-logs are pine milled flat on one side and rounded on the other. Then Stanley scoured flea markets for rustic furnishings and kitschy bric-a-brac—blankets, mini birch bark canoes, and vintage lake-theme art that were the souvenirs of bygone vacationers.

Exterior siding is painted a high-gloss brown for a varnished look. Inside, tongue-and-groove siding is nailed to the studs. Stanley replaced the home's fixed-panel windows with multipanes, and added birch trim to the screen porch. As he discovered, log-look siding is less expensive than building a log home or retrofitting an older home with real logs because an existing home's foundation must be bumped out to accommodate log width. The siding is available in various sizes and woods, including pine and cedar; some applications create a chinked effect with synthetic caulk. Stanley also reshaped the landscape, forging a natural connection to the woods with rock-edged ponds, footpaths, and gardens awash in the seasonal color of bulbs, perennials, and annuals. "You're only an hour and a half from Chicago, but it's a different world," he says.

make it
yours

Second homes beg for self-expression and a lighthearted touch. After all, your home's on vacation, too. Whitewash interiors for an endless summer mood, transplant a bit of Provence to the plains, or collect funky furnishings from a local flea market. Just relax your rooms and put comfort first. For inspiration, consider what drew you to that spot in the first place. The water? The woods? A tropical, seafaring, or Western mood? Anchor your getaway by letting the colors and materials of the region flow seamlessly inside. In this chapter, settings inspired the decorating that gives each retreat personality and a sense of place.

RIGHT: A herd of twig seating and colorful textiles personalizes the terrace of a Texas getaway overlooking the Brazos River.

AT HOME ON THE RANGE

art Ponderosa and part Daniel Boone, Rocky Top Ranch draws its design inspiration from the rough-and-ready spirit that won the West. The rugged Texas setting with commanding views of the Brazos River gives Rocky Top an authentic edge, but the creativity of homeowners Ron and Deborah Hall keeps guests guessing: Is it new or remodeled? That's a high compliment for the couple who designed and built their new weekend home using locally quarried stone and ideas from vernacular architecture. Inside, they rustled up comfortable, ranch-worthy rooms with cowboy memorabilia, and early-Texas and American country treasures.

OPPOSITE: The great-room's mix of antique and new Western furnishings creates ranch-style comfort. **TOP RIGHT:** A reproduction chair sports a gunfighter's silhouette. **ABOVE and RIGHT:** Ron and Deborah Hall play with pets, Possum and Daisy, at their new fieldstone-and-cedar retreat.

Cowboy poetry readings, team roping contests, and cookouts are on Rocky Top's weekend agenda when the Halls entertain. With movie-set precision, they roughed up the backdrops and decorated rooms with enough rugged charm to make modern-day cowpokes feel comfortable pulling off their boots and putting their feet up. Wide planks panel walls, and rough-bark cedar adds decorative Western style, inside and out. In the great-room, split-cedar logs frame windows and doors.

"We used stains and washes on everything. We mopped the ceiling with stain so it would look all soot," Ron says. "The craftsmen and carpenters thought we were mad. They couldn't understand why we would build something new and make it look so old."

OPPOSITE: Cowboy-style spreads and wagon-wheel windows and headboards accent the guest room. **ABOVE:** 1940s cowgirl photos and a wagon-wheel chair add a Western "twang." **ABOVE RIGHT:** Boots, chaps, and hats line the

HAPPY TRAILS STYLE

Lasso the cowboy look for your retreat with attention to detail.

❖ Accent to boot. Display big and little cowboy boots on shelves, and place hats and chaps on hall trees or walls. Use spurs as curtain tiebacks.

❖ Collect kitsch. Look for new or old Western-motif pieces, such as horse-head lamps and wagon-wheel chairs.

❖ Raid the chuck wagon. Display or set the table with vintage Westward Ho dinnerware and cowboy cups.

❖ Top beds with cowboy-motif spreads; use Beacon blankets as spreads, throws, or cushion covers; upholster with faux cowhide prints and leather.

The couple has been collecting Western furniture and accessories for some time, so the prospect of filling their rooms was a joy, not a problem. In fact, as their home was being built, they couldn't resist hitting the trail again to find even more unique pieces. "We went to flea markets and bought cowboy pieces," Deborah says. "Things we spent $2 and $5 for are now selling for $65 and $85."

Their collections range from 1930s and 1940s salt-and-pepper shakers and 1950s Roy Rogers kiddie cups to Westward Ho dinnerware, antique quilts, and Wild West art. Of course, to create the mood of a working ranch, they accented with items from the well-dressed buckaroo's closet—old cowboy boots in every size, worn chaps, spurs, and hats. One of the couple's favorite treasures is a custom pair of boots autographed by Dale Evans and Roy Rogers. To supplement collections of rustic furniture and farmhouse antiques, the Halls added some new Western oak pieces, but had them crafted in the Old West tradition of famed furniture designer Thomas Molesworth so they would fit into the mix. The Western theme blends new and old fabrics, too. Bronco-busting prints cover decorative pillows, and upholstery is done in cowhide-painted canvas, blanket-style fabrics, and leather. The Halls didn't miss a chance to serve up extra helpings of ranch dressing. The kitchen cabinetry has rope-look trim, and the island has a tin countertop. Made of recycled tractor seats, horseshoes, plow discs, and drill pipes, the barstools are a creative collaboration between Ron and a local blacksmith.

ABOVE: A blacksmith crafted tractor-seat barstools for the kitchen's tin-top island, set with Westward Ho dinnerware. **RIGHT:** An antique bed and quilts take this guest room back in time. Big multipane windows invite the outdoor scene inside.
OPPOSITE: Lined with rugged tree-branch railings, the sunny porch off the guest quarters provides visitors a spot for enjoying the swing, the view, and privacy.

NauTICaL BLUES

OPPOSITE: Wide overhangs and old wicker make the ocean-view porch a relaxing spot rain or shine. **ABOVE:** Whitewashed wainscot and nautical accents set the stage for seating slipcovered in easy-care denim. **RIGHT:** This 1910, shingle-style retreat takes design and color inspiration from the sea, sand, and sky.

Almost every window frames Nantucket Sound, ribbons of beach, and cloud-dappled skies, so Rita and Bob Davis decided that they'd found their expert decorator. Who could improve upon Mother Nature's palette? Seascapes that wrap their rambling, 1910 getaway inspire artists to grab their brushes and canvas. The couple drenched the interiors of the shingle-style classic with the soothing colors of sea, sand, and sky, then enhanced the seafaring mood with nautical accents. "We wanted more of a beachy, Cape Cod kind of feel to it," Rita says. "Everything is casual and relaxed." Comfy, no-fuss furnishings free up the couple's time for important things—fun with their three children and friends who stop out for weekend lobster boils and sailing.

NATURALLY NANTUCKET

Bring home the beach with colors and textures that instantly relax your rooms, and look around your seaside setting for even more inspiration.

■ Freshen up with paint. True blues, neutral hues, and creamy whites create backdrops that welcome treasures collected from antiques shops or beachcombing. Spray-paint old wicker for use inside or on the porch.

■ Warm up with texture. Mellow woods, twiggy wreaths, shells, weathered oars, anchors, and other nautical gear are natural accents. Beachy-looking sisal area rugs are practical because they sift sand through to the floor so it's not tracked around.

■ See the light. White-painted shutters, canvas Roman shades, or bamboo blinds make it easy to control the light and give windows a clean, unfussy look.

■ Take it easy with fabrics. Canvas, denim, sailcloth, and washable cottons with sea motifs, from seashell and fish prints to cabana stripes, make nautical mood setters for slipcovers and toss pillows.

■ Accent artfully. Collect seascapes and beach-theme art from flea markets or antiques shops, and check out the works of local artists.

To set an airy mood and highlight the original high ceilings, heavy moldings, and oak floors, the walls wear sandy beige or blue paint. Once-dark wainscot gleams, thanks to a coat of crisp white. With a good shake, washable denim slipcovers shed sand from the beach. Whether it's a ship model for the mantel or Windsor-style dining room chairs, Rita picks new pieces with muted colors, worn finishes, and classic lines for an old look that blends vintage finds from yard sales, antiques shops, and the attic.

OPPOSITE: A model ship accents the original stone fireplace between living room seating areas. **LEFT:** Blues link a medley of floral, striped, and seashell-print fabrics. **ABOVE:** A 9-foot-long dining table offers plenty of room for entertaining the weekend crowd.

OPPOSITE: A chambray spread and pillows cozy up the four-poster in the master bedroom that opens to a balcony. **ABOVE:** Beadboard walls and ceiling give the master bath a beachy feel. **RIGHT:** Nautical-print curtains with rope ties hang from an old oar-turned-rod. In front of the window, a mini lighthouse radiates seashore style.

Going with a fitting nautical theme made decorating a breeze, and investing time in do-it-yourself projects, such as painting porch wicker, sewing accent pillows and curtains, and refinishing furniture, made it a labor of love for the family. "Since it was casual, it was easy to go into antiques stores and find a pair of boat oars, or pick up different kinds of shells at another store," Rita says. "The nautical things always catch my eye, and I've been collecting them for 20 years." Remodeling changes were minimal, but the Davises did steal closet space to create the new master bath.

INTO THE WOODS

Deep in the Maine forest, winters call for buckling on snowshoes or cross-country skis, and summers for fishing and tubing on the lake. When it's time to stow the gear and head inside for a fireside supper, the destination for Bob and Barbara Schneider's family is a small-but-smarter version of the traditional Maine camp. Instead of dark, cramped, one-room living, however, the Schneiders' 1,100-square-foot lake home doubles the fun with two "cabins" in one open, airy floor plan that divides public and private areas and features high-volume spaces and sun-catching windows. To put their home at ease among the towering oaks and maples and blueberry bushes, they wrapped the exterior in Eastern white-cedar shingles and leafy-green trim, then carried forest colors, natural-finish woods, and rugged stone indoors to make living spaces inviting for the family and their guests.

OPPOSITE: The twin-cabin design of this Maine retreat tucks bedrooms on the private side. **ABOVE LEFT:** Built-in seating turns this "window box" into a reading spot. **ABOVE RIGHT:** Living room furnishings focus on the granite-face fireplace. Built-in cabinetry holds the entertainment center and library.

With gable-end, awning windows and a bumped-out "window box" with its own pitched roof and window seat in the living room, this new-generation cabin is sunnier than the typical camp. Carefully carved "view slots" through the tall trees keep the lake in sight from the home's interior living spaces.

"We wanted to be able to make wonderful memories right away," Barbara says. "It has a sense of magic to it, just a timelessness. It's so calming."

In the living room, a palette of forest greens and neutral hues ties together the diamond-pattern area rug, floral-print cushions on the cottage-style futon sofa, and accents, such as collectible pottery and pillows. Packing amenities into such a small space isn't always easy, but here, one wall does it all. The fireplace, soaring to the ridgepole, lines up with a built-in entertainment center/library on the living room side. Birch cabinetry fills the wall's kitchen side. A hallway leads to the sleeping quarters—two bedrooms separated by a bath—that mirror the lofty ceilings and sunny ambience of the living room.

ABOVE LEFT: New-but-nostalgic furnishings, such as the spindle bed and slat-back rocking chair, cozy up one bedroom. **OPPOSITE:** Crisp, lake-blue linens pop against the white walls and a pickled-cedar ceiling.

FOREST FLAVOR

Anchoring your cabin to its woodsy setting means looking to nature for building materials, color inspiration, accent textures, and low-maintenance landscaping ideas.

▧ Finish it naturally. See-through and pickled finishes on furniture, paneling, and cabinetry keep things light and allow pretty wood grains to show through.

▧ Rough it up. Rugged stone finishes, wicker baskets, and chairs with woven and caned seats add warm texture.

▧ Pick woodsy colors. Lake blues, leafy greens, earthy browns, and the golds and scarlets of fall tie interiors to the views.

The easy pace of lake life has this outdoorsy family looking forward to weekends when they can get some exercise, catch a few fish, and entertain friends at picnics and barbecues. The compact kitchen is deceivingly hardworking with high-efficiency appliances, a bistro-table dining spot, and enclosed storage for a pantry and washer and dryer. For mosquito-free entertaining, the screen porch has a drop-leaf table for snacks or small buffets and plenty of seating. The table is handy for board and card games, too. When the couple's son, Jackson, hosts sleepovers, the youngsters "camp out" on the screen porch and spread their sleeping bags wall to wall.

TOP: Living spaces and the screen porch open onto a lake-view, courtyard deck.
ABOVE: The L-shape kitchen's birch cabinetry has Shaker-style simplicity.
RIGHT: The screen porch extends living space with old-fashioned wicker seating.

SIMPLY Breezy

When rooms are "wallpapered" with ocean views, and you'd rather spend more time on the deck and at the beach than cleaning up inside, keep the decorating simple. At their cottage on Massachusetts' Plum Island, Kay and Jack McKallagat splashed on ocean blues and greens with sunflower-yellow accents against bright white backdrops. It's flip-flop style, as lighthearted as a day in the sun. "It's casualness. It's ease," Kay says. "It's easy on the eyes and easy to maintain." For that on-vacation feeling, they pared accents and picked furnishings for comfort and character.

LEFT: Kay McKallagat relaxes on the deck with daughter, Jesse, and pet, Sophie. **ABOVE:** This rattan chair and ottoman got the nod because they bespeak ease and add seaside character. **OPPOSITE:** Laid-back living room seating gathers around an old pine kitchen table shortened to coffee-table height.

As painters were finishing the new home, Kay liked how the primed walls enhanced the sunlight, and she made a color change. She substituted bright white on the walls instead of the planned linen hue. Coir area rugs cover natural birch floors, adding a beachy texture while also sifting sand to the floor. Furnishings, picked strictly for comfort, include a charming mix of attic and antiques shop finds and spiffed-up oldies from the couple's landlocked home that's more traditional in style. Somehow, Kay says, living at the beach inspired her to try light-look interiors for the first time, and now the family loves the look. Under the new canvas slipcover and reclad pillows, who would guess that the living room star is a worn yellow damask sofa? Put your feet up; it's washable.

LEFT: The dining table is made of old pine planks on a new base. **TOP RIGHT:** The kitchen has brushed stainless-steel countertops. **RIGHT:** Jesse plays with Sophie and Henry on a bench with a dune view.

With family and guests traipsing in and out and down to the beach, easy-care was the criterion for choosing fabrics and finishes, such as the epoxy-coated kitchen cabinets that wipe clean and brushed stainless-steel countertops that don't show scratches. "Everything in this house—every collection, every surface, every floor—has to do with low maintenance and practicality," Kay says.

She whittled down collections to a hardworking few—quilts for beds, pitchers that double as vases, and shell prints and old Plum Island scenes that reflect the home's colors and seaside setting. To maintain the clean, uncluttered spaces, the family votes on any new furnishings and accents.

OPPOSITE: This old chaise lounge in the master bedroom has fresh upholstery and a cushion of cotton fabric. **ABOVE:** A leggy dressing table from a junk store gets a little striped "tutu." **ABOVE RIGHT:** The oak bed has an unclad duvet and a dust ruffle made from striped linen dish-toweling that Kay bought inexpensively by the yard.

REFRESHING BEACH SPIRIT

Summer-style decorating conveys a relax-and-get-comfortable attitude. Here's how to put your own second-home rooms at ease.

▨ Breathe easy. Choose washable fabrics in sun-bleached colors—canvas, cottons, and even linen dish-toweling fill the bill—and forget busy patterns. Let sail-white walls and cool wood or tile floors play up a mix-and-match "wardrobe" of easygoing rugs, pillows, and artwork. At windows, keep fabrics light, designs simple.

▨ Edit, edit, edit. Don't clutter rooms with more than you need.

▨ Cover up. Restyle an old sofa from home for its new life at the beach by adding a new slipcover that pops off for cleaning.

▨ Mix casually. Unmatched furniture boosts a room's character.

romance ON THE RIVER

LEFT: The Mississippi River flows by the cottage, once a log cabin stop for 1800s French traders. **ABOVE:** Painted finishes accent the marble fireplace.

As dawn washes watercolor pastels over the misty river and the quaint cottage on its banks, the scene is a French Impressionist's dream, but the setting is really the Midwest. Mary Anne and Tom Thomson love the Provence region of France, but weekending there proved, well, impossible. So they turned a Mississippi River cottage—just 65 miles from their St. Louis home—into a French country retreat for weekends.

During the 1800s, local brick replaced the cottage's original logs and a second story was added, but the 1,200-square-foot home was vacant and dilapidated when the Thomsons saw possibilities, not just boarded-up windows. The 10-year makeover has been what Mary Anne calls "an affair of the heart." Gently, they turned imperfections into assets, gathered antiques and collections in unpretentious settings, and brushed watercolor hues over the interiors.

"Our challenge was not to 'fix it' perfectly and obliterate its history, but to celebrate its age, and let it tell a story," Tom says.

Mary Anne collects "whatever fills me with joy," and her signature mismatched decorating adds to the French feeling.

OPPOSITE: Leather chairs and a decoupaged table gather at the living room fireplace, finished to mimic raw concrete. **ABOVE:** Candles light the dining room brightened with fabrics. **ABOVE LEFT:** A kitchen sill holds an organic display of herbs and vinegars.

OLD-WORLD WAYS

If it's old-world ambience you're after, it's your call on how far you roam. Do you love French country? Do you yearn for the English countryside? How about a bit of Italy? Decorating can give your getaway the illusion of faraway places, without the need for passports.

■ Mix, don't match. Pick furniture and accents because you love each one to make rooms look like they evolved over time. It's the layering of worn, mismatched finds that creates the look.

■ Celebrate age. Faded Oriental rugs, old wrought-iron chandeliers, chipped gilt frames, a scuff here and there on a chair, and worn paint add character.

■ Create special effects. Mary Anne's flowing window curtains are made of "frugal French"—a linen-cotton blend that cost $1 a yard.

By mixing stand-alone pieces regardless of pedigree, rooms have an accumulated-over-time look. Few things are French in origin. With a candlelit, wrought-iron chandelier, golden walls, 1950s chairs, and a rustic table laden with bright-hued dishes and cloths, the dining room looks as if it were plucked from a farmhouse in the south of France. The stone-look floor is old painted pine, and window frames retain layers of old paint.

OPPOSITE and ABOVE: The master bedroom mixes a mid-1800s Victorian bed with a Hepplewhite slant-top desk and English chair. **LEFT:** An 1800s Italian puppet brings personality to the library.

FAR LEFT: An early 1800s washstand, layered with aged paint, conveys a sense of history. A handful of fresh-from-the garden blooms brings the vignette to life, as does the old hat rack, complete with vintage-style straw hats. **ABOVE:** This whimsical plaster hand offers—what else?—hand towels in the bath. The old wood floors, newly scrubbed but still displaying decades of wear, offer fuss-free charm under foot. **OPPOSITE:** Dressed in checkered spreads and handcrafted pillows, the guest room enjoys a scenic river view. An avid gardener, Mary Anne warms and colors each room with flowers all summer long.

Mary Anne's romantic rooms reflect her joie de vivre, and she doesn't hesitate to inject whimsy, such as the large antique marionette that oversees the library, or a hearth-side sculpture of a child holding a baseball bat and ball. She added wooden turtle doves to the old Victorian bed in the master bedroom.

"Anything that adds to life's simple pleasures is what I love," she says. Through the day, the river scene changes. As the couple tends their herb, vegetable, and flower gardens, or tackles another do-it-yourself project, a lazy parade of boats and barges glide by.

PATRIOTIC FLAIR

A desire for seaside life and the liberty to pursue summertime fun led Fred and Patti Lau to snap up this 1906 Coronado Island, California, cottage five minutes after they met it. With an all-American picket fence, graceful gambrel roof, and wide porch, this beach retreat is an icon in the island's architectural history. More than that, it offers the Laus a chance to make some family history of their own, too.

"We wanted a family gathering place—a place to create memories for our children and our grandchildren," says Patti, who designed clean, uncluttered interiors as fresh as an ocean breeze.

ABOVE: Flag-waving pillows by a quilt artist soften front-porch seating. **RIGHT:** Antique roses romance the arbor. **OPPOSITE:**The cottage is on the July 4th parade route, so it's dressed for the occasion.

Family and guests want to spend time strolling the beach, quaint shops, or the farmer's market, so the family declared independence from housekeeping with easy-care decorating. Informal antiques, rustic pine, and comfy new pieces mix with porchy wicker, indoors and out. Nobody frets about the dogs or kids tracking in sand because overstuffed seating is slipcovered in sturdy denim and sailcloth that pop into the wash. Painted backdrops are Patti's favorite butter yellow hue and white, and sisal rugs that clean with a good shake top hardwood floors.

TOP: Cheery colors wrap the breakfast room. **LEFT:** Family pets Oreo and Annie find the home's marine theme relaxing. **OPPOSITE:** The slipcovered sofa welcomes colorful, easy-to-change accents. After the Fourth of July, floral pillows replace flag motifs.

OPPOSITE and RIGHT: Wicker and easy-care fabrics, such as ticking, turned the boathouse into a home. **ABOVE:** Beachcomber finds, including weathered buoys, add a nautical accent.

Decorating with laid-back summer-house colors gives the family an artistic free hand in adding Americana collections and changing accents to fit the season. Grouped shells, framed seascapes, model ships, and buoys and other boating memorabilia anchor interiors to the island setting. When Independence Day rolls around, stars-and-stripes pillows replace everyday floral ones. "What started as a summer cottage has evolved into a haven used throughout the year," Patti says.

For guests, a dormitory upstairs opens to a balcony. The favorite hangout for the couple's children and their friends is the home's remodeled old boathouse.

SEASONAL PERSONALITY

Whether you live in endless summer or an area with dramatic seasons, quick-change decorating freshens the look. Start with neutrals, then:

■ Zip on style. Depending on fabrics, washable slipcovers can warm up, cool down, or give a room new perspective.

■ Pile on personality pillows made of novelty or seasonal fabrics.

■ Layer simple window valances or lengths of fabric over blinds, shades, or shutters for quick-to-change color and pattern.

THE WHITE WAY

When empty-nesters Grace and Bill Shanley searched for a building site on Connecticut's coast, they didn't stop at water's edge. Perched on rocks that once held a boathouse, their carefree retreat extends out over the water. "It's almost as though the house is floating," Grace says. "In this house, the view is the story." Every room captures it with French doors, and open spaces offer see-through views. The architecture honors New England nautical traditions, but inside, the home is comfortably contemporary with guest quarters for their grown children's visits.

LEFT: This Connecticut home-on-the-rocks replaced a Victorian-era boathouse. **ABOVE:** The kitchen has glass doors and open shelves to keep everything within easy reach and sight. **ABOVE RIGHT:** The stairway has a lighthouse newel post. **RIGHT:** Adjacent to the kitchen, the low-maintenance living room offers spectacular views of boats on Long Island Sound, making a telescope a must.

With such dramatic views, the couple kept interiors cool and understated with clean-lined furnishings and neutral backdrops and fabrics. Oriental rugs and decorative pillows provide the color shots, and Grace accents with artworks, including her own. For architectural interest, new beams top the foyer stairway that leads to her studio, and salvaged beams from the old boathouse unite the kitchen and living room. The kitchen has vintage details, such as a stone floor and beadboard-paneled cabinetry.

ABOVE and LEFT: In the bedroom, pale backdrops and white bed linens and slipcovers let the view dominate. **OPPOSITE:** Oak beams above the stairway anchor upper-level gallery space.

ABOVE: The house is built to withstand Nor'easters and the occasional hurricane with steel I-beam supports, hurricane-proof windows, and marine paint. **BELOW and OPPOSITE:** Bill Shanley's Long Island Sound vistas include boats and native grasses.

EMPHASIZING THE VIEW

When you want views of the setting to rule at your getaway home, consider quiet interiors with neutral colors and decorate with simplicity and restraint.

▨ Do it white. Always as crisp as a ship's sail whipping in the breeze, white fabrics and white walls are naturally soothing and keep interiors from competing with scenery.

▨ Warm with texture. Although the palette is white, mix fabrics, such as white-on-white stripes and florals and textured neutrals, to give rooms warmth and interest.

▨ Inject color. Add occasional dots of color to a white scheme with rugs, pillows, artwork, and collections.

▨ Build architectural character. Multiple French doors and natural wood beams and trims forge links to land and sea.

▨ Use barely-there basics. Artful modern lighting and minimal window shades or blinds do their jobs discreetly.

sites & sources

Use these sources and search tips to find, build, remodel, and decorate your own second home.

American Resort Development
  Association
  202/371-6700
  www.arda.org

Intervac International
  800/756-HOME
  www.intervac.com

National Golf Foundation
  800/733-6006
  www.nfg.org

National Oceanic and Atmospheric
  Administration (NOAA)
  202/482-6090 Fax: 202/482-3154
  www.noaa.gov

North American Golf Directory
  www.golfdirect.com

Realtor.com
  www.realtor.com

SnowHouse—mountain real estate
  guide at SnowSource.Com
  www.snowsource.com/shouse.htm

U.S. Geological Survey
  Dept. of Interior
  12201 Sunrise Valley Drive
  Reston, VA 20192
  www.usgs.gov

Search the Internet, using keywords,
  such as "getaway homes," "golf
  developments," "lake developments,"
  "lake homes," "mountain homes,"
  "real estate resorts," "recreational
  homes," "resort homes," "second
  home locations," "vacation homes,"
  and "waterfront living."

HOME DESIGN, BUILDING, AND REMODELING INFORMATION

American Institute of Architects
  202/626-7300 Fax: 202/626-7426
  www.aiaonline.com

American Institute of Building Design
  800/366-2423 Fax: 203/227-8624
  www.aibd.org

Better Homes and Gardens® magazine
  800/374-4244
  www.bhg.com

Better Homes and Gardens® Special
  Interest Publications, including:
  Building Ideas, Home Plan Ideas, and
  Remodeling Ideas, sold on newsstands

Building Systems Council
  National Association of Home Builders
  202/822-0576
  www.buildingsystems.org

Home Builders Institute
  202/371-0600 Fax: 202/898-7777
  www.hbi.org

Log Home Links.com—Manufacturers,
  Furnishings, Tools, Information
  www.loghomelinks.com

Manufactured Housing Institute
  800/505-5500
  www.mfghome.org

National Association of Home Builders
  800/368-5242
  www.nahb.com

National Association of the
  Remodeling Industry
  703/575-1100 Fax: 703/575-1121
  www.remodeltoday.com

Search the Internet, using keywords, such
  as "barn homes," "cabin homes," "log
  homes" "kit homes," "manufactured
  homes," "modular homes," "panelized
  homes," "post-and-beam homes,"
  "precut homes," "prefabricated
  homes," and "timberframe homes."

HOME PLANS WEBSITES
www.allplans.com
www.alternativehomeplans.com
www.architecturaldesigns.com
www.archwaypress.com
www.bhg.com
www.classic-cottages.com
www.collectivedesigns.com
www.coolhouseplans.com
www.dreamhomesource.com
www.dreamplans.com
www.drummonddesigns.com
www.eplans.com
www.homeplan-network.com
www.homestyles.com

www.houseplan.com
www.houseplanforum.com
www.larryjames.com
www.lifestylehomedesign.com
www.marshallarchitecture.com
www.simplehome.com
www.uniteddesign.com
www.weinmaster.com

Search the Internet, using keywords, such
  as "architectural home plans,"
  "cabin plans," "cottage plans,"
  "home plans," "house plans," and
  "vacation home plans."

FURNISHINGS SOURCES & WEBSITES
Cabin Fever
  828/295-0520
  www.thecabinfeversite.com

Flat Rock Furniture at Frontera.com
  800/762-5374
  www.frontera.com

French Country Living
  800/485-1302
  www.frenchcountryliving.com

L.L. Bean Home
  800/221-4221
  www.llbean.com

LodgeCraft Rustic Furniture
  800/296-2032
  www.lodgecraft.com

Lodgepole Creations
  406/961-4705
  www.lodgecreations.com

Lost Moose Mercantile Company
  800/253-6466
  www.widerview.com

Maine Cottage Furniture
  207/846-1430
  www.mainecottage.com

Oh! Susannah Furniture Co.
  619/275-3234
  www.ohsusannah.com

Plow & Hearth
  800/627-1712
  www.plowhearth.com

Rocky Mountain Lodgepole Furniture
  800/827-9042
  www.logfurn.com

Rue de France
  800/777-0998

www.ruedefrance.com

Secret Mountain Furniture
417/683-3238
www.secretmtnboats.com

Shaker Workshops
800/840-9121
www.shakerworkshops.com

Smith & Hawken
800/776-3336
www.smithandhawken.com

Sturbridge Yankee Workshop
800/343-1144
www.sturbridgeyankee.com

Taos Furniture
800/443-3448
www.taosfurniture.com

The UnPainted Place, Inc.
612/285-5555
www.unpaintedplace.com

Tidewater Workshop
800/666-8433
www.tidewaterworkshop.net

Vermont Outdoor Furniture
800/588-8834
www.vermontoutdoorfurnitur.com

Waterfront Living
800/341-5280

Whispering Pines
800/836-4662
www.whisperingpines.net

Search the Internet, using keywords, such as "Adirondack furniture," "cabin furnishings," "cedar furniture," "cottage furniture," "country furniture," "cowboy furniture," "cabin furniture," "hickory furniture," "lodge furniture," "log furniture," "pine furniture," "rustic furniture," "Southwestern furniture," "unfinished furniture," and "Western furniture."

CREDITS

INTRODUCTION
Pages 4-5—The Magic of it All.
  Photographs: Doug Hetherington

CHAPTER ONE
Pages 6-15—The Big Woods.
  Photographs: Jenifer Jordan.

Regional editor: Nancy E. Ingram.
Pages 16-21—Sand and Sea.
  Interior designer: Lisa Vandenburgh.
  Photographs: Tom McWilliam.
  Stylist: Tricia Foley.
Pages 22-27—An Island Escape.
  Photographs: William Stites.
Pages 28-35—Lakeshore Getaway.
  Architect: Marc Margulies.
  Photographs: Eric Roth.

CHAPTER THREE
Pages 60-63—A Sound Investment.
  Architect: Brooke Girty Architectural Design & Planning. Interior designer: Pamela Christensen & Co.
  Photographs: Jeff McNamara.
  Regional editor: Hillary Maharam.
Pages 64-67—Working with City Hall.
  Architect: Tobin T. Dougherty, AIA.
  Photographs: Jay Graham. Interior designer: Susanna Noble, ASID.
  Regional editor: Helen Heitkamp.
Pages 68-71—Smaller and Smarter.
  Photographs: Laurie Black.
  Regional editor: Barbara Mundall.
Pages 72-77—Migratory Patterns.
  Interior photographs: Bill Holt.
  Family photographs: John Williams.
  Stylists: Sally Mauer and Hilary Rose.
Pages 78-81—In Tune with the Site.
  Designer: Becky Hollingsworth.
  Photographer: Mike Moreland.
  Regional editor: Ruth L. Reiter.
Pages 82-85—A Sense of Place.
  Architect: Mulfinger, Susanka, and Mahady Architects, Inc.
  Photographs: Susan Gilmore.

CHAPTER FOUR
Pages 86-93—A Narrow Escape.
  Architect: Sortun Vos Architects.
  Photographs: Mike Jensen.
  Regional editor: Trish Maharam.
Pages 94-99—Little Luxuries.
  Architect: Sarah Susanka.
Pages 100-103—Coasting Home.
  Architect: Stephen Blatt, AIA.
  Landscape Designer: Bill Phinney.
  Photographs: James Salomon.
  Stylist: Isabel Smiles.
Pages 104-109—Style on a Shoestring.
  Photographs: Jim Yochum. Architects: John Allegretti, AIA, and Greg Good.
  Regional editor: Elaine Markoutsas.
Pages 110-115—Logging On.
  Photographs: Tim Murphy.
  Regional editor: Mindy Pantiel.
Pages 116-119—Going Modular.
  Photographs: D. Randolph Foulds.
  Architect: Wayne Neale.
  Regional editor: Eileen Deymier.
Pages 120-125—Island Timberframe.
  Photographs: Laurie Black.

Designer: Christina Koons Baker.
  Regional editor: Lynda Turner.
Pages 126-127—Personality in Detail.
  Architect: Roger Taylor Panek, AIA.
  Home plan #2129, Archway Press, Inc.

CHAPTER FIVE
Pages 128-133—Developing a Vision.
  Architect: Priscilla Zimmerman.
  Interior designer: Barbara Rostad.
  Kitchen designer: Nancy Fortner.
  Photographs: Bill Holt.
  Regional editor: Trish Maharam.
Pages 134-139—Preserving the Past.
  Photographs: James Yochum.
  Regional editor: Elaine Markoutsas.
Pages 140-145—Winterizing a Summer Home. Landscape designer: George Hughes. Photographs: Jim Hedrich.
  Regional editors: Sally Mauer and Hilary Rose.
Pages 146-151—Bringing the Outside In. Architect: John Banks.
  Photographs: James Yochum.
  Regional editor: Elaine Markoutsas.
Pages 152-153—Adding a Sunroom.
  Architect: H. Ronald Walker, AIA.
  Photographs: King Au.
Pages 154-157—Opening Up the Interiors. Architect: Stephen Blatt AIA.
  Photographs: James Salomon.
  Stylist: Isabel Smiles.
Pages 158-161—Welcoming Guests.
  Photographs: James Yochum.
  Landscape designer: Wendy King.
Pages 162-165—Facelifting the Exterior. Landscape designer: Gunner Piotter. Photographs: Barbara Elliott Martin and James Yochum. Regional editors: Sally Mauer and Hilary Rose.

CHAPTER SIX
Pages 166-173—At Home on the Range. Photographs: Jenifer Jordan.
  Regional editor: Nancy E. Ingram
Pages 174-179—Nautical Blues.
  Photographs: Sam Gray.
Pages 180-185—Into the Woods.
  Architect: James A. Sterling, AIA.
  Photographs: James Salomon.
  Stylist: Isabel Smiles.
Pages 186-191—Simply Breezy.
  Photographs: Eric Roth.
  Regional editor: Hilary Maharam.
Pages 192-199—Romance on the River.
  Photographs: Colleen Duffley.
  Regional editor: Mary AnneThomson.
Pages 200-205—Patriotic Flair.
  Photographs: Ed Golich.
  Regional editor: Andrea Caughey.
Pages 206-211—The White Way.
  Architect: Bruce Beinfeld.
  Photographs: Tria Giovan.
  Regional editor: Bonnie Maharam.

INDEX

A

Activities and amenities, 46-49
Adirondack chairs, 34, 74, 116, 150, 151, 163
Advice on choosing a location. *See also* Financial advice
  amenities, 46-49
  atmosphere, 38
  before-you-sign considerations, 76
  climate, 85
  cost, 55-56
  crowds versus solitude, 44-45
  neighborhood check, 65
  psyche self-check, 14
  put yourself in the picture, 36
  retirement reality check, 52
  shopping the circle, 51
  style of your home, 40-41
  trying out locations, 38
  views and scenery, 42-43, 210
  walks, 39
  water and air quality, 80
  websites, 212
A-frame cottage, 4-5
Air quality, 80
Architects, 97
Atmosphere, 38

B

Beach retreats
  breezy decorating scheme inspired by, 186-191
  classic Cape Cod seaside home, 16-21
  modular construction for, 116-119
Building a second home
  architects and builders, 97, 157
  budget-stretching with do-it-yourself skills, 68, 70
  city hall's input, 65-66
  cottage on a Seattle waterway, 86-93
  home design websites, 212
  island home sites, 124
  Lake Michigan cottage, 104-109
  log homes, 110-115
  Maine waterfront cliffhanger, 100-103
  modular construction, 116-119
  precut timberframe bungalow, 120-125
  smart design for limited square footage, 94-99, 104-109
  variations to change the exterior style of standard home plans, 126-127

C

Chalet variation of basic home design, 126, 127
Climate, 85
Colors for your cottage exterior, 132
Contractors, 157
Cost of a second home, 55-56. *See also* Financial advice
Crowds versus solitude, 44-45

D

Decorating inspired by settings. *See also* Homes shown in this book
  breezy beach cottage, 186-191
  Connecticut home-on-the-rocks, 206-211
  forest retreat in Maine, 180-185
  nautical scheme for Nantucket Sound, 174-179
  Old world ambience along Mississippi River, 192-199
  patriotic flair for island cottage, 22-27, 200-205
  Western style, 166-173
Decorating tips. *See also* Decorating inspired by settings; Remodeling advice
  beach spirit, 191
  cowboy look, 171
  creating room to breathe, 27
  emphasizing the view, 210
  forest flavor, 182
  furniture websites, 212-213
  fuss-free living, 18
  Old-world ambience, 197
  planning for a crowd, 31
  seasonal quick-change decorating, 205
  small spaces that live big, 91
  staying in tune with nature, 82-85

E

Exterior colors, 132
Exterior facelifts, 162-165

F

Farmhouses
  outdoorsy update for 1913 farmhouse, 146-151
  preservation of 1830 farmhouse, 134-139
Financial tips
  budget-stretching with do-it-yourself skills, 68, 70
  cost-effective modular construction, 116-119
  investment protection, 63
  mortgages, 56
  rental properties, 55, 56
  smart design for limited square footage, 94-99, 104-109
  taxes, 55
Fixing up your home. *See also* Home remodeling tips
  opening up interiors, 154-157

exterior facelift for '50s ranch, 162-165

guest quarters, 158-161

kit-built log cabin renovation, 128-133

1913 farmhouse update, 146-151

1934 cabin update, 6-15

preservation of 1830 farmhouse,
134-139

summer-only to year-round cottage,
140-145

sunrooms, 152-153

two-story addition for 1920s bungalow,
60-63

Flood insurance, 55, 76

Fun activities, your idea of, 46-49

Furniture websites, 212-213

Fuss-free living, 18

G

Getaway classics. *See also* Homes shown
in this book
beach house, 16-21
cabin in the woods, 6-15
island cottage, 22-27
lakeshore retreat, 28-35

H

Hobbies and second homes, 14

Home-based businesses, 52

Home building websites, 212

Home remodeling tips
choosing a contractor, 157
colors for your cottage exterior, 132
leaving well enough alone, 139
questions before remodeling, 150
winterizing a summer home, 144

Home plan websites, 212

Home renovation examples
additions for opening up interiors,
154-157
exterior facelift for '50s ranch, 162-165

guest quarters, 158-161

kit-built log cabin renovation, 128-133

1913 farmhouse update, 146-151

1934 cabin update, 6-15

preservation of 1830 farmhouse,
134-139

summer-only to year-round cottage,
140-145

sunrooms, 152-153

two-story addition for 1920s bungalow,
60-63

Homes shown in this book
beach cottage on Massachusetts' Plum
Island, 186-191
classic Cape Cod seaside home, 16-21
Connecticut home-on-the-rocks,
206-211
cottage on a Seattle waterway, 86-93
farmhouses, 134-139, 146-151
island cottages with patriotic flair,
22-27, 200-205
Lake Michigan cottage, 104-109
lakeshore home in NewHampshire,
28-35
lakeside retreat in northern Michigan,
72-77
log cabin renovation on Bainbridge
Island, Washington, 128-133
log home in Colorado, 110-115
Maine forest retreat, 180-185
Maine waterfront property, 100-103
marshland cottage in South Carolina,
78-81
Minneapolis architect's refuge, 95-99
Mississippi River cottage in Missouri,
192-199
modular beach house, 116-119
Nantucket Sound 1910 shingle-style
retreat, 174-179
north-woods cabin, 82-85

Oklahoma vintage cabin, 6-15

Oregon home built with budget-
stretching skills, 68-71

precut timberframe bungalow, 120-125

Western (Texas-style) ranch, 166-173

House-hunting considerations
activities and amenities, 46-49
atmosphere, 38
before-you-sign considerations, 76
climate, 85
cost, 55-56
crowds versus solitude, 44-45
distance and affordability, 51
neighborhoods, 65
proactive searching, 70
psyche and a suitable home, 14
retirement reality check, 52
style of your home, 40-41
trying out locations, 38
views and scenery, 42-43, 210
water and air quality, 80
websites, 212

I-K

Internet search tips, 212-213

Island getaway homes
breezy beach cottage, 186-191
1920s bungalow with two-story
addition, 60-63
patriotic flair for, 22-27, 200-205
precut timberframe bungalow, 120-125
renovated log cabin, 128-133

Island sites, building on, 124

L

Lakeshore getaways
Lake Michigan house, 104-109
New Hampshire home, 28-35
northern Michigan home, 72-77

Landscaping, maintenance-free, 18

Location of your second home
activities and amenities, 46-49
atmosphere, 38
before-you-sign considerations, 76
climate, 85
cost, 55-56
crowds versus solitude, 44-45
neighborhoods, 65
psyche self-check, 14
put yourself in the picture, 36
retirement reality check, 52
shopping the circle, 51
style of your home, 40-41
trying out locations, 38
views and scenery, 42-43, 210
visual quizzes, 39-43, 45, 48-49
water and air quality, 80
websites, 212

Log homes
custom, 110-115
kit-built log cabin topped with an
addition, 128-133
vintage 1934 cabin in the woods, 6-15
Log siding, 162-165

M-Q
Modular construction, 116-119
Mortgages, 56
Nature, decorating in tune with, 82-85
Nautical scheme, 174-179
Old-world ambience, 192-199
Patriotic flair for island retreats
with country furnishings, 22-27
with nautical accents, 200-205
Quizzes, 39-43, 45, 48-49

R
Remodeling advice
choosing a contractor, 157

colors for your cottage exterior, 132
leaving well enough alone, 139
questions before remodeling, 150
upgrading summer home for-
year-round comfort, 144
websites, 212
Remodeling examples
additions to open up interiors, 152-157
exterior facelift for '50s ranch, 162-165
guest quarters, 158-161
kit-built log cabin renovation, 128-133
1913 farmhouse update, 146-151
1934 cabin update, 6-15
preservation of 1830 farmhouse,
134-139
summer-only to year-round cottage,
140-145
sunroom addition, 152-153
two-story addition for 1920s bungalow,
60-63
Rental properties, 55, 56
Retirement homes, 52

S
Scenery, 42-43, 210
Second-home furniture, 212-213
Second-home locations. *See also* Homes
shown in this book
island, 22-27, 200-205
lake site, 28-35, 72-77
seashore, 16-21
woods, 6-15
Settings and decorating schemes
beach cottage, 186-191
Connecticut home-on-the-rocks,
206-211
forest retreat, 180-185
nautical scheme for Nantucket Sound,
174-179
Old-world ambience along Mississippi

River in Missouri, 192-199
patriotic flair for island cottage, 22-27,
200-205
Western style, 166-173
Solitude versus crowds, 44-45
Style of your home, 40-41
Sunrooms, 153

T-U
Taxes, 55
Texas-style comfort, 166-173
Timberframe bungalow, precut, 120-125

V
Victorian variation of basic home
design, 126, 127
Views and scenery, 42-43, 210

W-Z
Waterfront properties
beach cottage on Massachusetts'
Plum Island, 186-191
classic Cape Cod seaside home, 16-21
lakeshore getaway in New Hampshire,
28-35
lakeside retreat in Michigan, 72-77
Maine cliffhanger, 100-103
marshland cottage in South Carolina,
78-81
Mississippi River cottage in Missouri,
192-199
tri-level cottage on a Seattle waterway,
86-93
Visual quizzes, 39-43, 45, 48-49
Water quality, 80
Weather, 85
Websites, 212-213
Western style, 166-173
Winterizing a summer home, 140-145